INTERNATIONAL DEVELOPMENT IN FOCUS

The Impact of School Infrastructure on Learning
A Synthesis of the Evidence

Peter Barrett, Alberto Treves,
Tigran Shmis, Diego Ambasz, and Maria Ustinova

© 2019 International Bank for Reconstruction and Development / The World Bank
1818 H Street NW, Washington, DC 20433
Telephone: 202-473-1000; Internet: www.worldbank.org

Some rights reserved

1 2 3 4   21 20 19 18

Books in this series are published to communicate the results of Bank research, analysis, and operational experience with the least possible delay. The extent of language editing varies from book to book.

This work is a product of the staff of The World Bank with external contributions. The findings, interpretations, and conclusions expressed in this work do not necessarily reflect the views of The World Bank, its Board of Executive Directors, or the governments they represent. The World Bank does not guarantee the accuracy of the data included in this work. The boundaries, colors, denominations, and other information shown on any map in this work do not imply any judgment on the part of The World Bank concerning the legal status of any territory or the endorsement or acceptance of such boundaries.

Nothing herein shall constitute or be considered to be a limitation upon or waiver of the privileges and immunities of The World Bank, all of which are specifically reserved.

Rights and Permissions

This work is available under the Creative Commons Attribution 3.0 IGO license (CC BY 3.0 IGO) http://creativecommons.org/licenses/by/3.0/igo. Under the Creative Commons Attribution license, you are free to copy, distribute, transmit, and adapt this work, including for commercial purposes, under the following conditions:

Attribution—Please cite the work as follows: Barrett, Peter, Alberto Treves, Tigran Shmis, Diego Ambasz, and Maria Ustinova. 2019. *The Impact of School Infrastructure on Learning: A Synthesis of the Evidence.* International Development in Focus. Washington, DC: World Bank. doi:10.1596/978-1-4648-1378-8 License: Creative Commons Attribution CC BY 3.0 IGO

Translations—If you create a translation of this work, please add the following disclaimer along with the attribution: This translation was not created by The World Bank and should not be considered an official World Bank translation. The World Bank shall not be liable for any content or error in this translation.

Adaptations—If you create an adaptation of this work, please add the following disclaimer along with the attribution: This is an adaptation of an original work by The World Bank. Views and opinions expressed in the adaptation are the sole responsibility of the author or authors of the adaptation and are not endorsed by The World Bank.

Third-party content—The World Bank does not necessarily own each component of the content contained within the work. The World Bank therefore does not warrant that the use of any third-party-owned individual component or part contained in the work will not infringe on the rights of those third parties. The risk of claims resulting from such infringement rests solely with you. If you wish to re-use a component of the work, it is your responsibility to determine whether permission is needed for that re-use and to obtain permission from the copyright owner. Examples of components can include, but are not limited to, tables, figures, or images.

All queries on rights and licenses should be addressed to World Bank Publications, The World Bank Group, 1818 H Street NW, Washington, DC 20433, USA; e-mail: pubrights@worldbank.org.

ISBN: 978-1-4648-1378-8
DOI: 10.1596/978-1-4648-1378-8

Cover photo: @Tigran Shmis, Central Space of Aurora School, Espoo, Finland. Used with the permission of Tigran Shmis. Permission required for reuse.
Cover design: Debra Naylor / Naylor Design Inc.

Contents

Preface   *v*
Acknowledgments   *vii*
About the Authors   *ix*
Executive Summary   *xi*
Abbreviations   *xv*

CHAPTER 1: Introduction   **1**
   Context   1
   Methodology   2
   References   3

CHAPTER 2: Access to Education Infrastructure   **5**
   Introduction   5
   Optimal size of schools   5
   Class size and density   6
   Learning spaces and educational technology   8
   Implications for equity   9
   Summary   10
   Notes   11
   References   11

CHAPTER 3: Safe and Healthy School Buildings   **13**
   Introduction   13
   Impact on pupils   13
   Impact on teachers   14
   Scale of the problem   15
   Equity implications   15
   The dynamics at play   16
   Summary   17
   References   18

CHAPTER 4: Baseline Conditions for Learning   **21**
   Introduction   21
   Evidence for the impact of particular factors on learning   22
   Evidence of holistic impact of school spaces on learning   23
   Summary   28
   Notes   29
   References   29

CHAPTER 5: Links between School Design and Pedagogy and Community   33
Introduction   33
Pedagogy and space   33
Improving schools and increasing community wellbeing   36
Summary   38
Notes   39
References   39

CHAPTER 6: The Process of Effective Planning and Implementation   41
The need for dialogue   41
The need for ambition   42
The need for inspiration   43
The need for a long-term, holistic perspective   43
Summary   44
Notes   45
References   45

CHAPTER 7: Summary and Conclusions   47
Summary   47
Implications for future practice   49
Implications for future research   50
Conclusions   51
Reference   51

Box
3.1   OECD earthquake seismic safety recommendations   14

Figures
1.1   Learning environments for better educational outcomes   2
4.1   Contribution of each classroom measure   26
5.1   Learning interactions: Teacher, spaces, and pedagogy   35

Tables
4.1   Summary of literature reviews on the impact of school buildings on learning   22
4.2   Classroom characteristics that increase pupils' ability to learn   28

Preface

Governments and societies around the world strive to improve their education systems and ensure that all children and youths have the opportunity to go to school and acquire the knowledge and skills they need to lead healthy and productive lives. Key inputs to the education system, such as curricula, teachers, and education infrastructure, help to improve the quality of education.

The quality of education infrastructure, specifically its appropriate educational planning and design with a focus on child development, has been widely discussed in recent years. The Sustainable Development Goals[1], which are defined by the United Nations and scope the development agenda for all countries in the world, require countries to "build and upgrade education facilities that are child, disability and gender sensitive, and provide safe, non-violent, inclusive, and effective learning environments for all." Many stakeholders around the world are seeking evidence on how various learning settings may positively or negatively affect child development. The Inter-American Development Bank (IDB), Organisation for Economic Co-operation and Development (OECD), United Nations Educational, Scientific and Cultural Organization (UNESCO), Council of Europe Development Bank (CEB), and the World Bank are doing analytical work to answer the question of how to design schools that are efficient, inclusive, and conducive to learning. Moreover, the World Bank and other international financial institutions have large and diverse investment portfolios on school infrastructure in different parts of the world, amounting to billions of United States dollars. Therefore, there is a need for more evidence on the effectiveness of these educational infrastructure investments. The potential benefits of improving the spaces where education is provided can be sizeable, including energy savings, safer and healthier environments for children, and better learning outcomes.

Recent studies have shown that students' performance is enhanced in schools with better physical learning environments. As this report will show, the empirical argument for investing in learning environment is strong. Furthermore, although causal evidence on this topic is scarce, there is a growing number of non-experimental studies—many of them compiled here—that indicate that investments in quality school infrastructure are strongly associated with improved learning outcomes even after controlling for students' socioeconomic background and other relevant covariates. New technologies and emerging pedagogical practices have created new requirements for educational buildings. As a result, new approaches to building learning environments must be developed that both create better spaces for children and increase the efficiency of investments in educational infrastructure.

The planning of good learning spaces is a discipline that combines different sciences and that requires the involvement of all users of these spaces—teachers, parents, and children—in the decision-making process for infrastructure development. Policymakers could do more to include these groups in the envisioning, coordination, and planning of specific infrastructure projects.

The evidence base related to the impact of learning environments on academic outcomes is gradually growing across the world. Many studies are currently ongoing or are planned in various countries. We present this report as a contribution to the international dialogue on learning environments and as an input to the World Bank's educational infrastructure projects. The report consists of a thorough review of various studies of how physical school design affects the health, safety, and learning processes of children. The report's findings may be a useful input into project preparation in different countries, and we hope that it will stimulate greater collaboration on education topics among the various expert teams within the World Bank Group. However, our most important goal in initiating the preparation of this report was to identify the "unknowns" in terms of maximizing the efficiency of learning environments and to provide a foundation for a rigorous research program in this promising area.

NOTE

1. See https://www.un.org/sustainabledevelopment/sustainable-development-goals/ for more information.

Acknowledgments

The principal authors of this report are Peter Barrett and Alberto Treves. The report involved the conceptualization, review, and editing of the text carried out by a team of World Bank staff that included Diego Ambasz, Senior Education Specialist; Tigran Shmis, Senior Education Specialist; and Maria Ustinova, Education Consultant. The report team expresses their particular thanks to the peer reviewers of this report: Toby Linden, Practice Manager, Education Global Practice, East Asia and Pacific Region; and Michael Trucano, Senior Education and Technology Policy Specialist.

Guidance and support were provided by Cristian Aedo Inostroza, Practice Manager, Education Global Practice, South Asia Region; and Harry Anthony Patrinos, Practice Manager, Education Global Practice, Europe and Central Asia.

The most important role in the conceptual thinking behind this note and in the idea to publish this paper was played by the clients and partners of the World Bank in Argentina, Belarus, Peru, Romania, the Russian Federation, Serbia, and Uruguay. The commitment to education and the interest in creating better spaces for children demonstrated by our partners in these countries sparked many ideas in the team and eventually led us to sharing this knowledge and experience with other countries and the global community.

Special thanks to the editor Fiona Mackintosh for copyediting the report.

The document also benefitted from discussions with and guidance from Mary Filardo, Executive Director, 21st Century School Fund.

Finally, special thanks to the World Bank Publishing Program.

About the Authors

Diego Ambasz is a Senior Education Specialist in the Education Global Practice at the World Bank. He leads several education projects in Latin America and in Europe and Central Asia. In addition, he contributes with technical assistance for projects in other regions of the world. Prior to joining the World Bank in 2003, he held senior analytical and management positions in Argentina's public administration. His teaching experience in public policy included professor positions at the Santa Fe Catholic University in Argentina, San Martin National University in Peru, and Rosario National University in Argentina.

Ambasz is a PhD candidate in education at San Andres University in Argentina. He received an MA in economics and public policy from Di Tella University in Argentina. He has published several articles and papers on education and innovation policy. He is the coauthor of "Technology and Competitiveness in the MERCOSUR: Thoughts on the Development of a Pending Agenda."

Peter Barrett is a past President of the United Nations-established International Council for Research and Innovation in Building and Construction. He is Emeritus Professor of management in property and construction at Salford University in the United Kingdom and honorary Research Fellow in the Department of Education at Oxford University. Barrett is an International Advisor to the Organisation for Economic Co-operation and Development and the U.S.-based Academy of Neuroscience for Architecture and the American Institute of Architects.

More recently, Barrett has researched the theme of senses, brain, and spaces with an interest in school design and achieving optimal learning spaces. His findings have, for the first time, isolated the significant scale of the influence of physical classroom design on variations in pupils' learning.

He also provides strategic consultancy on optimizing the impact of school buildings on learning for the Norwegian Education Directorate, the World Bank in Romania, and for the Girls' Day School Trust and the Haberdashers' Aske's Boys' School in the United Kingdom, among others.

Tigran Shmis, a Senior Education Specialist, holds an undergraduate degree in computer science and economics education. He completed postgraduate study in information and communications technology and holds a PhD in education from the Russian Academy of Education. He later completed an MEd in education and educational policy at the Moscow branch of the University of Manchester. Shmis worked under educational projects in Belarus, Kazakhstan, Peru, Romania, the Russian Federation, and Serbia. Among those projects are the Yakutia Early Childhood Development (ECD) Project, Russian Education Aid for Development, and the Belarus Education Modernization Project. He also contributed technical assistance to the Safer Schools Development Project in Peru. He delivered several cooperation programs to the OECD Centre for Effective Learning Environments and the Early Childhood Education and Care networks, and to United Nations Educational, Scientific and Cultural Organization. Shmis leads work on innovative learning environments, ECD quality initiatives, and capacity building of the Russian Federation in international development aid in education.

Alberto Treves is a School-Building Specialist with more than 1,000 projects completed in the Americas, Africa, the Middle East, and Eastern Europe. He specializes in the early steps of the process, having created master plans, written design manuals and specifications, developed school designs, and advised governments and private institutions on capital improvement projects. He holds a master's degree in architecture from the University of Buenos Aires, and a certificate in educational facilities planning from the University of California, and he is a member of the Council of Educational Facility Planners International.

Treves has worked in many countries, and current and recent clients include the World Bank, Inter-American Development Bank, African Development Bank, United States Agency for International Development, Millennium Challenge Corporation, United Nations Educational, Scientific and Cultural Organization, Centro Regional de Construcciones Escolares para América Latina and other prestigious organizations.

Maria Ustinova is a Consultant at the World Bank office in Moscow, where she supports technical assistance and lending projects in the fields of education and social protection.

She also serves as an Associated Researcher at the Urban Health Games Research Group, which is part of the Architecture Department at the Technical University of Darmstadt, Germany. She contributes to research projects that investigate how urban planning and design influence human health and wellbeing, particularly focusing on school learning environments.

Ustinova holds double master's degrees in international cooperation and urban development from Darmstadt University of Technology, Germany, and University of Rome Tor Vergata, Italy.

Executive Summary

BACKGROUND

The aim of this report is to review current research studies on how school infrastructure affects children's learning outcomes and to identify key parameters that can inform the design, implementation, and supervision of future educational infrastructure projects. At the same time, this document also aims to identify areas where the evidence is currently less strong and where there is the potential for the further exploratory work.

School infrastructure constitutes a large component of the World Bank's education investment projects. The Bank's World Development Report 2018 titled "Learning to Realize Education's Promise" stresses the importance of making schools work for all learners and focuses on the need to ensure the high quality of education. The report emphasizes the need to guarantee the efficient use of public resources in delivering the maximum benefits of education to all children.

To ensure that investments in school infrastructure achieve the maximum positive impact on learning, this report suggests that a comprehensive set of questions needs answers:

- Do all children actually have access to a place at school?
- Do the school buildings provide a safe and healthy environment?
- Are the existing learning spaces optimally designed for learning?
- Does the design of the school foster current pedagogy and community engagement?
- How can the school infrastructure be designed to evolve sustainably over the longer term?

This report brings together the key findings from studies of international practice as a first step towards finding optimal solutions to the issues raised by these questions and maximizing the benefits of school infrastructure.

ACCESS TO SAFE AND HEALTHY SCHOOL PLACES

We found that providing access not only to school places but also to spaces that are safe and healthy positively affects pupils' academic outcomes.

Chapter 2 of this report describes the key conditions for maximizing effective access to school places. This involves schools that are: locally distributed to maintain reasonable travel to school distances; relatively small; with relatively small classes and relatively low density of classroom occupancy; utilized for a reasonable school day length; and with optimal scheduling within the spaces to release capacity to maximize educational benefits.

In chapter 3, we present the evidence in support of schools that are soundly built to withstand natural disasters, that provide basic services and opportunities for outside play, and have good indoor environmental quality. These factors positively contribute to pupils actually attending and remaining healthy in school and, in the case of teachers, staying in their profession. Very often school buildings fall short in these respects, and when they do, the most disadvantaged pupils are often those who suffer most.

BETTER SPACES FOR LEARNING

Evidence presented in chapter 4 of this report shows that the physical characteristics of learning spaces have a significant impact on educational progress. The impact has been estimated to explain on the order of 16 percent of the variation in pupils' learning (Barrett et al. 2015a).

The review team found that the following all positively contribute to pupils' progress in learning:

- Good "natural" conditions such as lighting, air quality, temperature control, acoustics, and links to nature
- Age-appropriate learning spaces that offer flexible learning opportunities that pupils can adapt and personalize
- Connections between learning spaces that are easy to navigate and that may provide additional learning opportunities
- A level of ambient stimulation using color and visual complexity
- Schools that are designed from the inside out (classroom to school) so that each space meets the needs of its inhabitants
- Designs that take into account local climatic and cultural conditions.

Drawing back from the detail in this area, it does make intuitive sense that to learn in a good physical environment should not be uncomfortable, alienating, chaotic, or boring. The evidence indicates that there is potential for many existing schools to be upgraded very economically and for new schools to be designed in ways that facilitate the learning imperative.

MAXIMIZING THE BENEFITS OF PEDAGOGY AND THE SCHOOL-COMMUNITY RELATIONSHIP

In order to maximize the positive impacts of school infrastructure investments, there is emerging evidence that the "fit" between the physical layout of a school and pedagogical practice is important. There are also persuasive arguments that engaging a wide range of stakeholders can increase the value of the education being delivered.

Chapter 5 of this report emphasizes that the physical layout of schools can reflect the dynamic of pedagogical practice, either by creating new schools or by adapting existing schools to make them more spatially flexible so that over the long term they can support rather than impede the desired developments in pedagogical practice. This chapter also discusses the possible major benefits to be gained by taking the local community into account when designing and planning school infrastructure, although the evidence for these gains is not well developed as yet.

Chapter 6 emphasizes that the implementation of school infrastructure projects should ideally be based on an ongoing dialogue among multiple stakeholders in order to reap the full benefits of these projects in terms of learning outcomes. This dialogue should continue over the long term to encompass ongoing changes in demography and pedagogy.

IMPLICATIONS FOR FUTURE PRACTICE

Having a better shared understanding of how the design of school infrastructure affects educational outcomes is very useful for those doing education sector work. The evidence presented in this report shows that a wider range of salient factors can be addressed for the same amount of expenditure. This will make it possible to develop better projects and to meet the specific needs of the children and teachers in question, with positive impacts for educational outcomes. It will increase the efficiency of the resources invested in school infrastructure projects and will lead to more effective cooperation between the different specialists involved in the development of school infrastructure.

IMPLICATIONS FOR FUTURE RESEARCH

The range of issues covered in this report is based on the best evidence available at the time of the study. There is much to build on immediately, but further research would be valuable in the following areas:

- In relation to spaces that are conducive to learning (see chapter 4), there is strong evidence from studies in OECD countries about which factors are critical for achieving positive learning outcomes. However, further studies are needed to explore what kinds of spaces are best for learning in different climates and cultures.
- Cross-cultural, comparative impact evaluation studies would be valuable to explore the issue of the optimal provision of places through the choice of school disposition and size.
- The evidence for the importance of safe and healthy schools to promote learning is strong, but investigations are urgently needed into how to make this happen effectively in the context of existing country-level regulations.
- Case studies are showing the importance of matching the chosen pedagogy to the space arrangement, but large-scale research will be needed to confirm this.

- There are persuasive arguments in favor of the contention that involving the whole range of stakeholders in all of the different stages of school planning has a positive effect on outcomes, but comparative case studies are needed to further explore this area.
- Technology has an important role to play in education, but the technologies chosen need to be appropriate for each specific school pedagogical approach and learning environment. Therefore, more research needs to be done to align the use of technology with the needs of schools, including not only learning spaces but also school planning and construction as well.
- There is also a need to generate evidence from infrastructure projects implemented in different contexts: from low to upper middle-income countries as well as from schools in different geographical locations, and with students from different cultural backgrounds.

We hope that this report will support those working in educational facilities by giving them a better understanding of the value of better school facilities in improving educational quality and extending the reach of the education system. We also see this work as a good start in the direction of further research on how to increase investments in educational infrastructure in ways that will overcome current challenges and reap all of the potential benefits, particularly those related to learning.

REFERENCE

Barrett, P., Y. Zhang, F. Davies, and L. Barrett. 2015a. *Clever Classrooms: Summary Report of the HEAD Project*, University of Salford: Salford.

Abbreviations

AQ	air quality
BSF	Building Schools for the Future
CSR	Classroom Size Reduction
HEAD	Holistic Evidence and Design
IDB	Inter-American Development Bank
IEQ	indoor environmental quality
NAEP	National Assessment of Educational Progress
OCZ	outside their comfort zone
OECD	Organisation for Economic Co-operation and Development
PPP	public-private partnerships
SEN	special educational needs
STAR	Student Teacher Achievement Research
WDR	World Development Report

1 Introduction

CONTEXT

The positive benefits associated with creating an educated population are spelled out in the latest World Bank's World Development Report (WDR) entitled "Learning to Realize Education's Promise" (World Bank 2018). The report is built on the notion that education is a fundamental way to achieve development and growth. Thus, it is essential to design *educational infrastructure* in such a way as to maximize the accessibility and effectiveness of the education being delivered. The WDR also emphasized that the potential of education can only be realized if education policies are evidence-based and well-targeted and if the whole system is designed to foster high-quality learning.

The WDR stresses that the recent expansion of education does not guarantee the immediate achievement of important learning outcomes so more attention must be paid to measuring and improving the quality of learning. It also argues for the importance of developing the skills of both pupils and teachers to enable them to meet the demand for teachers in the future. This emphasis on future-orientated skills is in keeping with the Organisation for Economic Co-operation and Development's (OECD) learner-centered principles (Dumont, Istance, and Benavides 2010).

This report shows the evidence presented in different studies on the relationship between school infrastructure and academic outcomes.

In the first instance, several key questions need to be addressed:

- First, do all children actually have access to a place at school?
- Second, do the school buildings provide a safe and healthy environment?
- Third, are the learning spaces optimally designed for learning?
- Fourth, does the school's design facilitate pedagogy and community engagement?
- Fifth, how can the school infrastructure be developed in a sustainable way?

Policymakers and planners need to consider all five of these questions together in searching for optimal design solutions for school infrastructure investments. The following sections of the report will address each of these issues in turn and then draw overall conclusions.

METHODOLOGY

To prepare this report, the authors extensively reviewed 129 publications devoted to the built environment of schools, education policy, and the learning process, including academic articles, research reports, books, and monographs.

The narrative is organized in a format of a critical review, which provides an opportunity to "take stock [and] provide a launch pad for a new phase" of learning environments research by drawing material from diverse sources and traditions (Grant and Booth 2009). This has been achieved by a thorough analysis and synthesis of the information, leading to a set of propositions developed by the authors. The main selection criteria for the literature was to choose sources that derived knowledge from sound empirical evidence.

The findings were categorized and discussed according to the following dimensions, presented in the figure 1.1:

- The accessibility of the school
- Safety and health
- Optimal spaces for learning
- Synergy with the pedagogy and community
- The effective implementation of the school project.

Figure 1.1 shows the structure of the analysis in this report. A set of aspirations for schools (at the bottom of the diagram) generates a range of practical imperatives (at the top) and the text between summarizes the salient issues to be considered, for which the authors have identified evidence in the literature. Each section of this review relates to one of these dimensions.

FIGURE 1.1

Learning environments for better educational outcomes

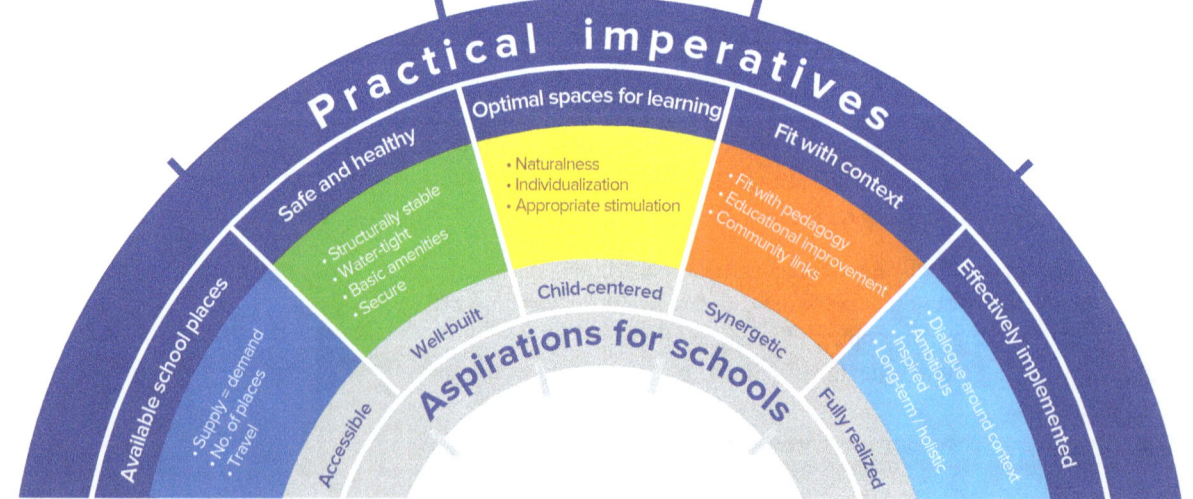

The field of educational facilities infrastructure draws on many disciplines, starting from architectural design and ergonomics and proceeding to education policy and pedagogy. Therefore, it was necessary to form an interdisciplinary review team. This team consisted of one school design practitioner with wide international experience and one academic researcher who specialized in the impact of school infrastructure on learning. This made the review process more robust and provided routes to two different, but complementary "libraries" of evidence built up over time. It also afforded the opportunity to explore and triangulate these perspectives around the emerging themes.

The following review is focused only on primary and secondary educational institutions, mostly situated in the United States, the United Kingdom, and Western European countries. As is implicit in this methodological approach, this report is not intended as an endpoint but as a starting point for further action. A key aspect of this is rooted in the fact that the great majority of the evidential studies are from the developed world. Therefore, there is a need for further work on exploring and testing the degree to which these essentially human-centric findings will need to be adapted when applied elsewhere, particularly in the developing world.

REFERENCES

Dumont, H., D. Istance, and F. Benavides, eds. 2010. *The Nature of Learning: Using Reseach to Inspire Practice*. Educational Research and Innovation. Paris: OECD Publishing.

Grant M. J., and A. Booth. 2009. "A Typology of Reviews: An Analysis of 14 Review Types and Associated Methodologies." *Health Information and Libraries Journal* 26: 91–108.

World Bank. 2018. World Development Report 2018: Learning to Realize Education's Promise. Washington, DC: World Bank. © World Bank. https://openknowledge.worldbank.org/handle/10986/28340 License: CC BY 3.0 IGO.

2 Access to Education Infrastructure

INTRODUCTION

School planners have always wrestled with the question of how to create a school (or a school system with buildings in different locations) that will best facilitate the educational process. Although not impossible, it requires a very clear vision of the current situation, of the expectations of all stakeholders, and the best possible path to meet these expectations. From the facilities point of view, it is always necessary to have some common quantitative denominators or parameters that will allow planners to detect any anomalies in the existing school or system and designers to come up with solutions that meet both current and long-term needs. Some of the most important parameters are school size and class size. These will be considered first in this section, followed by options for using space and issues of equity.

OPTIMAL SIZE OF SCHOOLS

For years in the USA the size of schools was mostly conditioned by an arguable concept of economics that considered that the larger the school, the lower the cost per student. An influential book written in 1959 by James Bryant Conant, (Conant 1959) President of Harvard University, called small high schools America's number one education problem, and many very large high schools were built based on the findings of that book. However, there is a lot of more recent evidence that small schools yield better academic results. The landmark 2002 report "Dollars and Sense: The Cost Effectiveness of Small Schools" (Bingler et al. 2002) examined 489 schools whose designs were submitted to design competitions between 1990 and 2001 and concluded that small schools can be built and operated cost-effectively according to a broad variety of measures.

The same study also mentioned that small schools are not effective solely by virtue of being small but rather work best when they take advantage of being small. The best small schools offer an environment where teachers, students, and parents see themselves as part of a community and deal with issues of learning, diversity, governance, and building in a home-like learning place.

The study found the most common drawbacks of larger schools were:

- Higher transportation costs
- Higher administrative overheads
- Lower graduation rates
- Higher absenteeism
- Higher rates of vandalism
- Lower teacher satisfaction.

In 2001, the evaluation (American Institutes for Research, SRI International 2005) of grants program provided to small schools in New York City that aimed to prepare low-income, African-American, and Hispanic youths for higher education and the workplace, found that students in these schools had more positive attitudes than students in more conventional schools. They felt more supported by their teachers, and they were more interested in their school work. They also had a 60 percent higher attendance rate than average, and students reported that they planned not only to graduate from high school but to apply to college at higher rates than students in other schools. A subsequent comparative, longitudinal study in 2010 (Bloom, Levy, and Unterman 2010) of these "small schools" in New York found that their pupils made academic progress that was significantly ahead of the students in the control group, who were typically in bigger and older schools. This effect was found in the first year of high school but continued right through to senior year, yielding greatly increased graduation rates.

Leithwood and Jantzi's (Leithwood and Jantzi 2009) major 2009 literature review on the question of school size looked back over 45 years of research but focused especially on the previous nine years' output. They concluded that smaller schools contribute positively to student outcomes, including higher student achievement, better attendance, higher graduation rates, and greater engagement in extracurricular activities. They also strongly suggested that these effects are more powerful in relation to disadvantaged children. Their conclusions regarding school size were that elementary schools should be limited to 500 pupils or, if serving a high proportion of disadvantaged pupils, then a maximum of 300 pupils. Their equivalent figures for secondary schools were 1,000 and 600 pupils. This impact on the socially disadvantaged, and especially for children with learning difficulties, was confirmed in a 2015 longitudinal study of schools in North Carolina (Gershenson and Langbein 2015), even though these schools were generally within the above size limits.

School size has geospatial implications. In a given geographical area, providing smaller schools means that they must be more locally distributed throughout the area according to the density of demand for places. To the extent that this reduces the distance that pupils have to travel to school, there can be real benefits to this approach. It has been found that extended travel times to get to school can have a range of negative effects on pupils and families, including the wasted time spent in transit and the reduced opportunity for pupils to take part in after-school activities or for their parents to engage with the school themselves.[1]

CLASS SIZE AND DENSITY

In Finland, which, according to the Program for International Student Assessment (PISA), has one of the highest education scores in the world, schools on average have only 195 students, with only 19 in each classroom

(Finnish National Board of Education 2016). The Ministry of Education's (Finnish Ministry of Education 2012) current thinking is that the potential of each student should be maximized by providing students with strong education guidance and by teaching them in small groups. This policy fosters a closer relationship between teacher and students, students and students, and between the community and the school and strengthens the commitment to education from all stakeholders.

There is strong evidence from around the world about the benefits of smaller classes, including better academic results (Blackmore et al. 2011; Brühwiler and Blatchford 2011).

The Tennessee STAR (Student Teacher Achievement Research) (Finn Krueger 2001) was carried out between 1985 and 1989. In this study, random students from kindergarten to third grade were placed in either small classes or large classes. The students in smaller classes, consisting of 13–17 students, scored 0.015 to 0.020 or about 5 percent higher than the students in the larger classes on standardized tests in both math and reading. This was particularly significant for students from kindergarten to third grade, and those benefits were carried on into higher grades.

Using a slightly different methodology, a study published by the Los Angeles Unified School District (Fidler 2001) showed that, with other parameters being equal, the longer a student is taught in smaller classes, the higher his or her achievement in reading and language. In general, larger gains were observed in mathematics, except for those students with limited English proficiency.

California's Classroom Size Reduction (CSR) Initiative of 1990, a state-wide effort to reduce classroom size, has been reviewed by many authors. In 2005, Faith Unlu from Princeton University (Unlu 2005) produced a study using data from the National Assessment of Educational Progress (NAEP), which contains comparable test scores prior to the program and afterwards for California and other states. Using a larger set of data, Unlu concluded that the CSR initiative had had a positive and significant influence on the achievement scores of California students. In particular, most specifications suggest that, between 1996 and 2000, California 4th graders' NAEP test scores in mathematics increased by between 0.2 and 0.3 of a standard deviation compared to the increase for closely matched students who were not included in the CSR initiative.

It has been suggested that to gain the full benefits of reduced class sizes and to change teaching practices towards more child-centered education, classes need to consist of 15–20 students (down from the 30 that is typical in the UK), but this can be quite costly (The Education Endowment Foundation Toolkit 2017).

Another related issue is the density of students in the classroom. Many researchers agree that overcrowded conditions hinder students' academic performance. A 1995 study of data collected by the New York Board of Education (Rivera-Batiz and Marti 1995) from 213 teachers and 599 students indicated that both teachers and students had expressed negative sentiments towards school overcrowding such as being overwhelmed, discouraged, and often disgusted. Many considered it to be the most serious issue facing the schools. The study also found that these sentiments were particularly strong in schools with a high proportion of students from low socioeconomic backgrounds where overcrowding was strongly linked with lower achievement.

Reinforcing this point, a study using an experimental methodology (Griffitt and Veitch 1971) demonstrated that uncomfortable environmental conditions such as high temperatures, high noise levels, and overcrowding can cause interpersonal disputes, hostility, and even violence, and this is also likely to be the case in classrooms.

One limitation of these studies is the typical understanding of a school classroom as fixed in space and a class as a defined number of students per one teacher. Currently, many countries are moving towards making their learning spaces and classes more flexible by piloting variable class sizes, team teaching, and small group work among other variations. Introducing flexibility into learning spaces can make teaching more efficient and make better and more efficient use of school facilities. There is a need for more research in this area, particularly about the opportunities and risks that these developments create.

LEARNING SPACES AND EDUCATIONAL TECHNOLOGY

Various factors influence the number of seats that are effectively available in a classroom, including technology and specific education programs, as well as the building's layout and constraints. Usually across the world students in kindergarten and the lower grades have a "home" classroom where they have most of their activities. If they occasionally go elsewhere for music, art, or outside learning, they always return to their "home" classrooms. In higher grades, the 9th grade and above, students often rotate between different subject classrooms, science laboratories, art workshops, library, and sport fields. In this case, different groups of students will use classrooms on a fixed schedule just as they use laboratories or music rooms. This rotation may make it possible for these more specialist classrooms to be used more frequently and efficiently, which could help to alleviate overcrowding situations in some schools. In many cases, when space permits, the flexible arrangement of furniture and equipment within spaces can also help students to acquire collaboration, teamwork, and other interpersonal skills. This is certainly an aspect of the evidence on the impact of "learning zones" (see "Evidence of Holistic Impact of School Spaces on Learning" section in chapter 4). Thus, the quality of education can be enhanced by appropriate planning, design, and patterns of operation in schools.

In recent years with the increasing use of technology-based content in the curriculum, students may spend more time out of the classroom. Educational IT can allow them to learn at their own pace in purposely designed break-out[2] spaces, outside learning areas, or even corridors, staircases, or cafeterias. Flexibility and adaptability in the design of formal and informal learning spaces may not only provide students with more diverse learning opportunities, stimuli, and experiences but also the chance to develop non-cognitive skills. However, this is not simply a matter of more technology or a belief that its use is good *per se*. The Organisation for Economic Co-operation and Development (OECD) (OECD 2015) carried out an international investigation into the impact of heavy investments in technology in schools in 2015 and came up with mixed findings. They found some evidence that moderate use of computers in the classroom tended to assist learning outcomes but also discovered some negative effects of heavy use of computers. One interpretation that the OECD gave was that "building deep, conceptual understanding and higher-order thinking requires intensive teacher-student interaction, and technology sometimes distracts from this valuable human engagement." They stressed that the use of technology must be fully aligned with the pedagogies being used in schools, and this itself is an area on which there are many contested views (see "Pedagogy and Space" section in chapter 5). This also reinforces the argument, stated above, that the school building has to be planned and designed primarily around educational requirements in order for it to be effective as a "third teacher."

This review is focused on the physical spaces and so will not pursue the topic of technology further, but it can be said that, in some ways, technology now takes up less space as there has been a shift in some countries from specialized computer labs to isolated desktops in the classroom, to mobile laptop trolleys, and to more freely available personal devices supported by wireless technology. As a result, it is not as difficult as it used to be in practical terms to have free access to computers (or phones), but it is very much a live issue as to whether it is always desirable.

While the number of "seats" in a school and how they are set out is of vital importance, the quantity of education delivered is also affected by the length of the school day. This varies widely from country to country. For example, in Romania, it is quite common for children to attend school for only half the day as part of a two-shift system (Barrett and Barrett 2016). In South Asia, despite figures indicating very positive increases in enrollment rates and gender parity among students (as indicated by the UN statistics), academic outcomes are still poor throughout the region (Asim et al. 2015). It would seem that a major reason for this is the short length of the school day in some countries in the region such as India where the school day typically lasts for only three hours compared to six to eight hours per day on average in OECD countries (Banerjee and Duflo 2011). In addition, there is evidence that starting the school day later, for adolescents especially, can be beneficial as it fits with their natural cycle of alertness during the day (Lockley 2015).

IMPLICATIONS FOR EQUITY

From a purely numeric outlook, classroom and school size are important elements of the facility planning process on the supply side. When compared with demand, this will show a deficit or surplus of available places in a given planning area. The difference between need and availability of places is the basis on which to determine a plan of new school construction, expansion, or renovation. There is robust evidence, for example in South Asia, that "school building programs rank among the most effective educational interventions." (Asim et al. 2015; Petrosino et al. 2012)

According to the Center for Public Education, (Center for Public Education 2016) equity is achieved in education when all students receive the resources that they need to graduate fully equipped to succeed after high school. Whether the goal is high school graduation, university success, or just to finish elementary school, policymakers aim to ensure an equal and fair distribution of the resources that students need to achieve their goals, including adequate school facilities, so that every member of each age group has the opportunity to attend school.

Equity is a universal goal with consequences for the building environment and includes:

- All genders
- People with special educational needs and disabilities
- Urban, rural, and marginal area populations
- Populations in transition
- Working children and youths.

For example, one of the basic principles of the education system in Finland is that all people must have equal access to high quality education and training (MacNeice and Bowen 2016). A similar mandate is found in the legislation of pretty much every country, but these laws are rarely fully implemented mostly because of budgetary constraints.

Achieving equity means that all schools should be safe from natural disasters or any other outside concerns and should have all of the spaces, furniture, and equipment needed to deliver the curriculum in an effective way. Conversely, inequity means a lack of or insufficient bathroom facilities, inadequate separation between boys and girls, long or dangerous walking distances to school, or, as also mentioned by Kathleen Cotton (Cotton 1996), the fact that many more poor students and those of racial and ethnic minorities have to attend larger schools than other students.

Another shameful form of inequity, is discrimination against students with disabilities as manifested by a lack of ramps, inadequate bathroom facilities, poor signage, and a lack of specialized teacher support. This kind of discrimination is a relatively easy problem to solve with adequate facilities that meet current design standards existing in most countries around the world.

Unequal distribution of educational resources creates frustration and resentment and in many cases school dropouts and teacher absenteeism. On the other hand, ensuring that schools have adequate facilities could play a definitive role in improving equity, increasing enrollment rates, and fostering student retention. World Bank professionals (Schady and Paxson 1999) concluded in a 1999 study that, in Peru, building and renovating school facilities had a positive effect on attendance rates.

SUMMARY

There is evidence that the following all have a positive effect on pupils' academic outcomes:

- Small schools
- Schools locally distributed to maintain acceptable travel distances to school
- Small classes
- Low density of classroom occupancy[3]
- Optimal school day length
- Optimal scheduling of the use of spaces to maximize educational benefit.

Each country and, in some cases, each province or district has its own parameters that are used in planning. These usually include two key measures: capacity[4] and utilization.[5] Both of these measures are likely to vary between regular classrooms, laboratories, and physical education facilities and also by educational level. This information is typically presented in codes or standards that are applied to all government-sponsored school construction. All of the particular elements described above should be discussed as part of a Facilities Master Planning process to identify challenges and establish priorities for the allocation of funds. As Mary Filardo (Filardo 2008) has advocated, this should be done according to explicit criteria that have been developed with input from the public. The aim of this planning process is to ensure that every member of a particular age group has the opportunity to attend a school that meets their expectations.

To conclude, there are many ways in which the design of educational facilities can enhance educational outcomes. Once these ways have been identified and taken into consideration in the planning and design process, this will provide a sound basis for extending educational provision to all.

NOTES

1. Private correspondence with Janssen Edelweiss Teixeira, Senior Education Specialist at the World Bank in Washington, based on a recent study of educational infrastructure in Romania.
2. Break-out spaces are spaces in the school building that are not designed primarily for classes and can be used by students to do individual work or small groups work (corners with sofas, nooks in the walls, or specially designed and furnished corridor space).
3. For example, a minimum of two meters per pupil is the norm in Norway, but 1.83 meters per pupil is typical in the UK.
4. *Capacity* is the number of seats available in a standard classroom multiplied by the number of classrooms and by the number of shifts that the school operates.
5. *Utilization* reflects the number of class hours during which a specific room is used per week divided by the number of hours a week that the room is used.

REFERENCES

American Institutes for Research, SRI International. 2005. https://docs.gatesfoundation.org/documents/year4evaluationairsri.pdf.

Asim, S., R. S. Chase, A. Dar, and A. Schmillen. 2015. "Improving Education Outcomes in South Asia: Findings from a Decade of Impact Evaluations." Policy Research Working Papers 73622015, The World Bank, Washington, DC.

Banerjee, A. V., and E. Duflo. 2011. E, "Why Aren't Children Learning?" *Development Outreach* (April): (13): 36–44. https://doi.org/10.1596/1020-797X_13_1_36.

Barrett, P., and L. Barrett. 2016. *Report on the Assessment of the Potential Impact of the Physical Condition of a Sample of Romanian Schools on Learning Outcomes*. Romania: International Bank for Reconstruction and Development/the World Bank.

Bingler, Steven, Barbara M. Diamond, Bobbie Hill, Jerry L. Hoffman, Craig B. Howley, Barbara Kent Lawrence, Stacy Mitchell, David Rudolph, and Elliot Washor. 2002. *Dollars and Sense: The Cost Effectiveness of Small Schools*, Concordia and KnowledgeWorks Foundation.

Blackmore, J., D. Bateman, J. Loughlin, J. O'Mara, and G. Aranda. 2011. *Research into the Connection between Built Learning Spaces and Student Outcomes*. Melbourne: Education, Policy and Research Division, Department of Education and early Childhood Development, State of Victoria.

Bloom, H. S., S. Levy, and T. R. Unterman. 2010. *Transforming the High School Experience: How New York City's New Small Schools Are Boosting Student Achievement and Graduation Rates*. New York: MDRC.

Brühwiler, C., and P. Blatchford. 2011. "Effects of Class Size and Adaptive Teaching Competency on Classroom Processes and Academic Outcome." *Learning and Instruction* 21 (1): 95–108.

Center for Public Education. 2016. *Educational Equity: What Does it Mean? How Do We Know When We Reach It?* http://www.centerforpubliceducation.org/system/files/Equity%20Symposium_0.pdf.

Conant, James Bryant. 1959. *The American High School Today*. McGraw-Hill, New York.

Cotton, K. 1996. "School Size, School Climate, and Student Performance," *Northwest Regional Educational Laboratory (NWREL)*. May 1996, Close-Up#20. https://educationnorthwest.org/sites/default/files/SizeClimateandPerformance.pdf.

Fidler, Penny. 2001. *The Impact of Class Size Reduction on Student Achievement.* Planning, Assessment and Research Division Publication No. 109, Los Angeles Unified School District.

Filardo, M. 2008. *Good Buildings, Better Schools: An Economic Stimulus Opportunity with Long-term Benefits.* Washington, D.C.: Economic Policy Institute. Briefing Paper #216.

Finn, Jeremy, and Alan Krueger. 2001. *Class Size: Project STAR.* American Youth Policy Forum.

Finnish Ministry of Education. 2012. *Education in Finland.* Helsinki.

Finnish National Board of Education. 2016. *Compulsory Education in Finland.* Helsinki.

Gershenson, S., and L. Langbein. 2015. "The Effect of Primary School Size on Academic Achievement." *Educational Evaluation and Policy Analysis* 37 (1S): 135S–55S.

Griffitt, W. and R. Veitch. 1971. "Hot and Crowded: Influences of Population Density and Temperature on Interpersonal Affective Behavior." *Journal of Personality and Social Psychology.* 1971 Jan; 17 (1): 92–8. Manhattan, KS: Kansas State University.

Leithwood, K., and D. Jantzi. 2009. "A Review of Empirical Evidence About School Size Effects: A Policy Perspective." *Review of Educational Research* 79 (1): 464–90.

Lockley, S. 2015. *Interventions to Improve Sleep, Alertness and Learning in Schools* in *Research Summit: Childhood Health and School Buildings.* Washington, DC: US Green Building Council, Dunbar Senior High School.

MacNeice, B. and J. Bowen 2016. *Powerhouse: Insider Accounts into the World's Top High-performance Organizations.* London: KoganPage.

OECD. 2015. *Students, Computers and Learning: Making the Connection.* Paris: OECD Publishing.

Petrosino, A., C. Morgan, T. A. Fronius, E. E. Tanner-Smith, and R. F. Boruch. 2012. "Interventions in Developing Nations for Improving Primary and Secondary School Enrollment of Children: A Systematic Review." *Campbell Systematic Reviews* 2012: 19.

Rivera-Batiz, F. L., and L. Marti. 1995. *A School System at Risk: A Study of the Consequences of Overcrowding in New York City Public Schools.* New York: Columbia University.

Schady, N. and C. Paxson 1999. *Do School Facilities Matter? The Case of the Peruvian Social Fund (FONCODES).* Washington, D.C.: World Bank.

The Education Endowment Foundation Toolkit. 2017. (accessed June 22, 2017), https://educationendowmentfoundation.org.uk/resources/teaching-learning-toolkit/built-environment/.

Unlu, Faith. 2005. *California Class Size Reduction Reform: New Findings from the NAEP.* Princeton University.

3 Safe and Healthy School Buildings

INTRODUCTION

Threats to the safety of schools can come from both inside and outside the school buildings. It is easy to imagine how distracting it would be for students, teachers, and parents if, for example, the school's structure may not withstand the next earthquake, or if its electrical wiring is exposed, its window glass is broken, or its bathrooms are a source of contamination instead of being sanitary. If school buildings are prone to be flooded by intensive rains, swept away by high winds, exposed to hazardous materials, or decaying for lack of maintenance, it hinders both teaching and learning, making it harder to produce the level of academic results that are possible in a safe and healthy building. This report centers on the physical environment and, although there are grave safety issues related to the safeguarding of pupils and staff from violent attack, this topic is beyond the scope of this review. The focus here is on fundamental physical conditions and does not extend to issues such as surveillance systems and security checks related to portals of entry and access to the school site.

IMPACT ON PUPILS

When Glen Earthman (Earthman 2004), an American educational administrator and planner, was asked to name the most important elements related to health and safety, he mentioned: potable water, fire safety, adequate lavatories, security systems, and a good communication system to use in emergencies. Research done in Latin America in 2011 (Duarte et al. 2011) showed that the lack of basic services such as electricity, potable water, sanitary drains, telephone or proper ways to dispose garbage and waste in schools is strongly associated with violence, discrimination, and limited opportunities to learn. The study pointed out that investments in school infrastructure and the physical conditions for learning are not a luxury but a need. In 2014, The Organisation for Economic Co-operation and Development (OECD) published a report highlighting seven key ways to protect schools from earthquakes, which in 2017 became a monitored framework (see box 3.1) (OECD 2017).

> **BOX 3.1**
>
> ### OECD earthquake seismic safety recommendations
>
> 1. Seismic safety policy
> 2. Accountability
> 3. Building codes and enforcement
> 4. Training and qualification
> 5. Preparedness and planning
> 6. Community awareness and participation
> 7. Risk reduction in new and existing schools
>
> *Source:* OECD 2017.

Many building-related factors influence the well-being of its occupants. Water and moisture can have a major impact on public health. A worldwide study by UNDP in 2006 found that children lose 443 million school days each year because of water-related illnesses (UNDP 2006), of which 272 million are lost due to diarrhea alone (Hutton and Haller 2004). More than 40 percent of diarrhea cases among schoolchildren are the result of transmission in schools rather than in their homes.

At a less extreme, but still very pervasive level, many researchers (US National Research Council 2006) have identified poor air quality as a source of health problems, with dampness causing the most absences from school (by both pupils and teachers) (Issa et al. 2011; Kielb et al. 2015; Mendell and Heath 2005).

In closed environments, respiratory problems seem to be the main cause of absenteeism. The US Environmental Protection Agency has estimated that more than 10 million days of schooling are lost each year in the US because of asthma attacks among students (U.S. Environmental Protection Agency 2000). Additionally, a study sponsored by the Centers for Disease Control in New York (Simons et al. 2010) found that moisture and dampness can cause the growth of mold and the proliferation of dust mites, which can produce allergic respiratory symptoms and foster infections. Poor ventilation enables particulates, pollutants, and allergens to accumulate inside school buildings, and inadequate air circulation can increase the transmission of respiratory infections. For example, a study of 409 classrooms in Idaho and Washington in 2004 (Shendell et al. 2004) found that student absences jumped by 10–20 percent in rooms with poor ventilation.

It is also important for students to spend time outside for recreation and physical activity. Several authors (Duarte et al. 2011; Sharif 2014) have concurred on the need for schools to provide recreational and physical education activities to balance the more intellectual school work as play has a significant impact on almost every aspect of children's development. However, schools are not always able to provide children with these opportunities. For example, in Latin American countries, 35 percent of students have no designated space to play sports in their schools, which is having serious negative consequences on learning outcomes in the region.

In urban areas, where land is scarce and green areas are in short supply, vertical gardens and "eco-trees" in courtyards could be developed to provide shade, natural cooling, and pleasant views. These sorts of initiatives would give students the chance to learn how to look after plants and seeing first-hand how they grow, are harvested, and recycled. Botany, physics, chemistry, biology, and other lessons could be held outside.

IMPACT ON TEACHERS

Teachers are not immune to health and safety concerns. Researchers (Chaudhury et al. 2006) from several lending institutions and universities made unannounced visits to primary schools in Bangladesh, Ecuador, India, Indonesia, Peru, and Uganda in 2006 and found that about 19 percent of teachers were absent. To try to understand this phenomenon, they constructed an index measuring the quality of the school's infrastructure that included whether the school had a toilet, covered classrooms, non-dirt floors, electricity, or a school library. The analysis for the sample as a whole suggested that: "moving from a school with the lowest infrastructure index score to one with the highest (that is, from a score of zero to five) is associated with a 10-percentage point reduction in teacher absence." This conclusion echoed the results of studies in 2004 and 2016 that found a strong relationship between US and UK teachers' perceptions respectively of the maintenance and condition of the buildings and their intentions to stay or leave the profession. The state of the infrastructure was found to be a more significant factor than their salary levels (Buckley, Schneider, and Shang 2004; Thomas and Pasquale 2016).

SCALE OF THE PROBLEM

In the view of the American Federation of Teachers (American Federation of Teachers 2008), conventional school construction often falls short of expectations, with teachers, staff and students often having to work in buildings with leaking roofs, inadequate ventilation, and other problems. For two decades, the American Federation of Teachers has been documenting the high cost of deteriorating schools. Students, teachers, and staff pay the price for these deplorable building conditions in the form of lower educational achievement, lost income, and health problems. The breakdown of America's education infrastructure exacts a heavy toll not only on those who spend their days inside school walls, but also on the environment in general. In the UK, a 2016 survey found that only 5 percent of 59,967 schools were "performing as intended." (Thomas and Pasquale 2016) The US and the UK are wealthy countries so it is not surprising that these school infrastructure and related problems are much worse in many other regions around the world (World Health Organization 2015).

EQUITY IMPLICATIONS

Glen Earthman's 2004 study (Earthman 2004) highlighted an important factor that needs to be considered when discussing the relationship between building conditions and student achievement—inequity. Earthman found that most older school buildings and those in poor condition are located in the poorest areas in each school district in both urban and rural areas. Students from poor areas, as a general rule, perform less well than students from more affluent areas. When low-income students attend school in a building that does not meet even basic safety and health standards, never mind the factors that have been proven to improve students' academic performance, then they are doubly disadvantaged. Also, the failure of education authorities to make improvements to a demonstrably old and failing facility can give these students the message that the system values them less than it does their counterparts in more affluent areas.

THE DYNAMICS AT PLAY

There are many issues interacting dynamically in practice. For example, is a school being adequately maintained over time? Even if standards set out in regulations are high, are new and existing buildings actually meeting those standards? Are teachers and school staff making pupil responsible for problems with the physical environment of their school (for example, a lack of cleanliness or dilapidation)? Are there day-to-day tensions between the competing needs of different users of the facilities? The education process relies heavily on the presence and the wellbeing of students and teachers. A child or a teacher who is sick or whose capabilities are diminished by environmental conditions is not capable of a fully productive engagement in educational activities. In his 2008 book, McDaniel College scholar Tom Zirpoli (Zirpoli 2008) found that when children misbehave or do not embrace their responsibilities, parents and caregivers frequently focus on assessing and identifying what may be wrong with the *child*. Both teachers and parents look for quick and easy answers to questions regarding children's inappropriate behavior. This blame-the-victim syndrome places too great an emphasis on how to "fix" children; instead, greater emphasis should be put on improving the quality of children's environments.

This can often be done by maintaining existing school buildings in good condition (fit for purpose) over the long term, including carrying out any necessary improvements and adapting them to meet changing educational needs. This kind of consistent maintenance, if reliably carried out in buildings that are fundamentally structurally sound, can result in a good quality educational environment in buildings of any age (Barrett, Barrett, and Zhang 2015). At the level of higher education, for many leading institutions, such as the Universities of Oxford and Cambridge in the UK or Harvard University in the US, their real estate is a key part of the nature of the institution, its image, and the experience of the students. Indeed, in the case of Harvard, the argument has been made that the evolving development of the estate very directly created the institution that exists today (Nason et al. 1949). This is a two-way process of course as the buildings have also been adapted to meet changing needs as must be the case if a building is to remain useful and relevant (Brand 1994).

In practice, buildings are often not maintained in good condition. This highlights the danger of assuming, just because there are good national regulations or standards, that these are enforced in the stock on the ground. For example, Higgins/Woolner et al.'s (Higgins et al. 2005; Woolner et al. 2007) statement in 2007 publication that there are clear links between "poor quality school buildings and classrooms and poor outcomes for learners ... and evidence that bringing [them] ... into the 'normal range' ... reverses the detrimental effect" (p. 50) has been erroneously interpreted (Education Endowment Foundation Toolkit 2017) to mean that there is no evidence of the impact of physical design, except at the extremes. We believe that this is a flawed interpretation as the impacts, for which there is a lot of evidence, are to be found within the very typical range of conditions of real UK schools (Barrett et al. 2015). Furthermore, a recent study came to the shocking conclusion that "environmental conditions in elementary schools are often inadequate, even in developed countries... thermal and air quality conditions are now almost universally worse than the relevant standards and building codes ... they are frequently much worse than in office buildings." (Wargocki and Wyon 2013)

Maybe in countries such as Norway (Barrett and Barrett 2016) and Denmark (Toftum et al. 2015) that use balanced ventilation systems, standards are generally high, but the problems are likely to be greater in many developing countries. In these countries, UNESCO (UNESCO Institute for Statistics 2012) has stressed that the real challenge is not the absence of set standards, but the implementation of those standards on the ground. It seems that this still applies in much of the developed countries' educational building stock too, including projects sponsored by the major lending and developing institutions.

Day-to-day there are other tensions at play, for example, the conflict between the need to save energy and the need for ventilation and light (US National Research Council 2006). Often teachers keep windows shut to save energy but cause poor air quality in the classroom as a result. As in office buildings, the negative impact on health and performance cannot be justified by the minor cost savings in energy use (Wargocki and Wyon 2013, 2017).

This tension could be resolved if the "green building" movement extends into the area of schools. As the US National Academies report in 2006 stated, after observing that the "green" emphasis tends to be on energy-saving: "Much is still not known about the potential interactions of building systems, materials, operation and maintenance practices and their effects on building occupants in general, or about school environments in particular." (US National Research Council 2006) Several studies have called for learning and health to be taken into account alongside environmental concerns (Baker and Bernstein 2012). Positively, a comparative Canadian study (Issa et al. 2011) found that, in green schools, teachers were in general more satisfied with their classrooms and personal workspaces (but were less satisfied with acoustics), that there was less student, teacher, and staff absenteeism, and that student performance was better than in non-green schools.

SUMMARY

There is strong evidence that the following factors all positively increase the chances of pupils and teachers attending school and remaining healthy at school and, in the case of teachers, staying in their profession:

- Schools that are soundly built and proof against natural disasters
- The provision of and access to basic services, such as water, sanitation, waste disposal, electricity, and communications
- Good indoor environmental quality, especially in relation to air quality and dampness
- Opportunities for outside play
- Schools that are maintained in good physical condition
- Regulations and standards that are enforced effectively on the ground
- Training that shows users how to get the maximum health and learning benefits from their school infrastructure.

These are quite basic aspirations, but our experience shows that school buildings often fall short and that, when they do, it is often the most disadvantaged who get the worst provision. UNESCO has found that most countries have sound regulations for school building, so the focus needs to be on the effective implementation of these standards in every country and region. This could be supplemented with initiatives to share good practices between different countries and regions, such as the OECD's report on earthquake safety that was aimed at informing developing countries as well as the World Bank's Safer Schools program (see also "The Need for Inspiration" section in chapter 6 for a range of international design examples). Along the same lines, it is also worth mentioning the eight multi-author documents published by the Interamerican Development Bank (IDB) on 21st century schools with the description of challenges and solutions from Argentina, Chile, Colombia, the Dominican Republic, Honduras, Jamaica, and Mexico (Gargiulo 2014).

REFERENCES

American Federation of Teachers. 2008. *Building Minds, Minding Buildings*. Washington, DC.

Baker, L., and H. Bernstein. 2012. *The Impact of School Buildings on Student Health and Performance: A Call for Research*. New York: McGraw-Hill Research Foundation.

Barrett, P. and L. Barrett. 2016. *HEAD for Norway: Knowledge Transfer Project for School Design for Learning*. Buxton, UK: Nutbox Consultancy. http://www.skoleanlegg.utdanningsdirektoratet.no/uploads/Artikler_vedlegg/FOU/HEAD%20for%20Norway%20Report%20-%20Final.pdf.

Barrett, P., L. Barrett, and Y. Zhang. 2015. "Teachers' Views of their Primary School Classrooms." *Intelligent Buildings International* 8: 1–16. https://doi.org/10.1080/17508975.2015.1087835.

Barrett, P. S., F. Davies, Y. Zhang, and L. Barrett. 2015. "The Impact of Classroom Design on Pupils' Learning: Final Results of a Holistic, Multi-Level Analysis." *Building and Environment* 89: 118–33.

Brand, S. 1994. *How Buildings Learn: What Happens After They're Built*. New York: Penguin Books.

Buckley, J., M. Schneider, and Y. Shang. 2004. *The Effects of School Facility Quality on Teacher Retention in Urban School Districts*. Washington, DC: National Clearinghouse for Educational Facilities.

Chaudhury, N., J. Hammer, M. Kremer, K. Muralidharan, and F. H. Rogers. 2006. "Missing in Action: Teacher and Health Worker Absence in Developing Countries," *Journal of Economic Perspectives*, 20 (1): 91–116

Duarte, J., C. Gargiulo, and M. Moreno. 2011. *Infraestructura Escolar y Aprendizajes en la Educación Básica Latinoamericana: Un Análisis a Partir Del SERCE*. Washington, D.C.: International Development Bank.

Earthman, G. 2004. *Prioritization of 31 Criteria for School Building Adequacy*. Baltimore, MD: ACLU.

Gargiulo, Carlos. 2014. *Learning in Twenty-First Century Schools*. Washington, DC: Interamerican Development Bank.

Higgins, S., E. Hall, K. Wall, P. Woolner, and C. McCaughey. 2005. *The Impact of School Environments: A Literature Review*. London: Design Council.

Hutton, G. and L. Haller. 2004. *Evaluation of the Costs and Benefits of Water and Sanitation Improvements at the Global Level*. Geneva: World Health Organization.

Issa, M. H., J. H. Rankin, M. Attalla, and A. J. Christian. 2011. "Absenteeism, Performance and Occupant Satisfaction with the Indoor Environment of Green Toronto Schools." *Indoor and Built Environment* 20 (5): 511–23.

Kielb, C., S. Lin, N. Muscatiello, W. Hord, J. Rogers-Harrington, and J. Healy. 2015. "Building-Related Health Symptoms and Classroom Indoor Air Quality: A Survey of School Teachers in New York State." *Indoor Air* 25 (4): 371–80.

Mendell, M., and G. Heath. 2005. "Do Indoor Pollutants and Thermal Conditions in School Influence Student Performance?" *Indoor Air* 15: 27–52.

Nason, T. W., S. Chamberlain, W. M. Rittase, W. R. Fleischer, and S. E. Morison. 1949. *Education Bricks and Mortar*. Cambridge, MA: Harvard University. p. 100.

OECD. 2017. *Protecting Students and Schools from Earthquakes: The Seven OECD Principles for School Seismic Safety*. Paris: OECD.

Sharif, S. 2014. *School Playground: Its Impact on Children's Learning and Development*. Bangladesh: Institute of Educational Development, BRAC University.

Shendell, D. G., R. Prill, W. J. Fisk, M. G. Apte, D. Blak, D. Faulkner. 2004. "Associations Between Classroom CO2 Cconcentrations and Student Attendance in Washington and Idaho," *Indoor Air* 14 (5): 333–341.

Simons, E, S. -A. Hwang, E. F. Fitzgerald, C. Kielb, and S. Li. 2010. *The Impact of School Building Conditions on Student Absenteeism in Upstate New York*. Washington, D.C.: National Library of Medicine, National Institutes of Health.

The Education Endowment Foundation Toolkit. 2017. (accessed June 22, 2017), https://educationendowmentfoundation.org.uk/resources/teaching-learning-toolkit/built-environment/.

Thomas, J., and L. A. Pasquale. 2016. *Better Spaces for Learning*. London: RIBA.

Toftum, J., B. Kjeldsen, P. Wargocki, H. Mena, E. Hansen, and G. Clausen. 2015. "Association between Classroom Ventilation Mode and Learning Outcome in Danish Schools." *Building and Environment* 92: 494–503.

UNDP. 2006. *Raising Clean Hands: Advancing Learning, Health and Participation through WASH in Schools*. New York: Human Development Report: Beyond Scarcity: Power, poverty and the global water crisis.

UNESCO Institute for Statistics. 2012. *A Place to Learn: Lessons from Research on Learning Environments*. Montreal: UNESCO.

US Environmental Protection Agency. 2002. *IAQ Tools for Schools: Managing Asthma in the School Environment*. Washington, D.C.

US National Research Council. 2006. *Green Schools: Attributes for Health and Learning*. Committee to Review and Assess the Health and Productivity Benefits of Green Schools. Washington, DC: The National Academies Press.

Wargocki, P., and D. Wyon. 2013. "Providing Better Thermal and Air Quality Conditions in Classrooms Would Be Cost-Effective." *Building and Environment* 59: 581–89.

———. 2017. "Ten Questions Concerning Thermal and Indoor Air Quality Effects on the Performance of Office Work and Schoolwork." *Building and Environment* 112: 359–66.

Woolner, P., E. Hall, S. Higgins, C. McCaughey, and K. Wall. 2007. "A Sound Foundation? What We Know about the Impact of Environments on Learning and the Implications for Building Schools for the Future." *Oxford Review of Education* 33 (1): 47–70.

World Health Organization. 2015. *School Environment: Policies and Current Status*. Copenhagen: WHO Regional Office for Europe.

Zirpoli, T. 2008. *Behavioral Management*. Westminster, MD: McDaniel College.

4 Baseline Conditions for Learning

INTRODUCTION

The question of the positive and negative effects of school design on academic outcomes has been studied by a lot of researchers. Their efforts have revealed a modest relationship between students' exam results and their subjective satisfaction with the condition of their facilities (Hopland and Nyhus 2015). What is not clear is which aspects of school facilities these pupils are taking into account. For instance, the correlation between the student satisfaction and satisfactory technical condition measures of the building is low, so the satisfaction with the learning environments has clearly a deeper dimension than just an infrastructure condition.

So, this is a knotty problem, especially as there are so many other factors in play, not least the tremendous variation in the characteristics and abilities of the pupils and in what is happening in their lives outside of school. Despite this complexity, there is a growing body of evidence focused on specific aspects of school facilities, such as air quality (AQ). Some of this work has been carried out in laboratories while other studies have focused on users' perceptions within the classroom. The volume of this evidence is impressive and cumulatively persuasive.

These research results are a very significant foundation for future initiatives as they provide insights into and reasons why various design elements are important. Because they were mostly carried out by specialist researchers, they have the advantage of depth but the problem of limited scope as defined by the disciplines involved. However, there is an increasing recognition that users experience spaces holistically and dynamically, leading to a recent drive towards studying multiple factors together (Kim and de Dear 2012). In this kind of research, the focus is sometimes on combinations of the most readily measurable factors such as temperature and light, while other recent work has successfully taken a top-down, user perspective. Through this combination of approaches (Barrett and Barrett 2003), real progress is beginning to be made towards answering crucial questions.

TABLE 4.1 **Summary of literature reviews on the impact of school buildings on learning**

AUTHOR/DATE	TITLE	METHOD	MAIN FINDINGS/FUTURE WORK
Schneider 2002	Do School Facilities Affect Academic Outcomes?	Literature review of 137 sources	The review found that spatial configuration, noise, heat, cold, light, and air quality all affect learning. However, more definitive findings are needed.
Woolner et al. 2007	A Sound Foundation? What We Know About the Impact of Environments on Learning and the Implications for Building Schools for the Future	Team literature review of 200+ sources	The review found clear evidence that extremes of environmental elements affect learning but not as much once the elements are raised above minimum standards. It strongly recommended to involve users in the process of change. However, overall, there was not enough empirical evidence to inform the design of future infrastructure projects.
US National Research Council Committee 2006	Green Schools: Attributes for Health and Learning	Team literature review of 392 sources (general—applied to green design).	Generally, the review found that pupils' health and learning were positively affected by good indoor air quality, thermal comfort, good acoustics, well-maintained systems, and clean surfaces. The study's main focus on health highlighted problems associated with excessive moisture. More research is needed at the individual level of analysis.
Blackmore et al. 2011	Research into the Connection between Built Learning Spaces and Student Outcomes	Literature review of 700+ varied sources	The review found very little empirical evidence specifically linking design elements of learning spaces to student outcomes. The review found that studies tended to over-emphasize the design stage and not pay enough attention to how it interacts with users, to the dynamics of implementation, or to the relevance of the design to types of educational practice.
UNESCO Institute for Statistics 2012	A Place to Learn: Lessons from Research on Learning Environments	Literature review of 91+ sources	The basics of IEQ are well known, but the "learning environments research" field is developing rapidly. However, its conclusions are hard to apply in practice outside the developed world.
Davies et al. 2013	Creative Learning Environments in Education: A Systematic Literature Review	Literature review of 210 sources (including how the physical environment affects creativity)	The review highlighted the importance of light, color, sound, and micro-climate in engendering creativity but also space, flexibility, the availability of resources, and links to outside actors. It stresses the link between design elements and pedagogical issues such as how to strike the right balance between freedom and structure in learning.
Bluyssen 2016	Health, Comfort, and Performance of Children in Classrooms	Literature review of 100+ sources	The review found evidence that design elements have affected learning, absenteeism, and, mainly, health. It concluded that there is a need for more experimental and/or longitudinal research with parameters for children.

Note: IEQ = Indoor Environmental Quality.

In this section, we continue reviewing the evidence on how school design features affect outcomes, specifically learning, which is the core purpose of any educational institution. The section starts by discussing baseline Indoor Environmental Quality (IEQ)[1] factors and then extends to other important factors. We have considered many different individual studies in this analysis as well as seven large literature reviews published between 2002 and 2016. These reviews are briefly summarized in table 4.1.

EVIDENCE FOR THE IMPACT OF PARTICULAR FACTORS ON LEARNING

The IEQ factors focus on the readily measurable "big four"—light, AQ, temperature, and acoustics. All seven literature reviews consistently found that all four of these factors have an effect on academic outcomes in schools.

There are a number of other points to add:

- There is a tendency to see daytime lighting as good *per se*, as a functional way to see well enough to read. There is also an increasing awareness of the non-visual impact of light on people's circadian rhythms and alertness (US National Research Council 2006). Furthermore, researchers are paying more attention to the impact of dynamic variations in lighting (Wessolowski et al. 2014) and the type and quality of artificial light sources (Barkmann Wessolowski and Schulte-Markwort 2012). It is also the case that daylight can be associated with glare and overheating and so ensuring shade where necessary is crucial or the effects can quickly become negative.
- Air quality is generally measured using CO_2 levels as a surrogate for the freshness of the air. CO_2 itself is not poisonous (Bluyssen 2016), but there is strong evidence that poor AQ as indicated by higher CO_2 levels reduces students' ability to concentrate and perform in tests (Shaughnessy et al. 2006; Wargocki and Wyon 2007). Recent Scandinavian studies have reinforced the educational value of good AQ (Toftum et al. 2015; Toyinbo et al. 2016).
- There is a comfortable temperature range for humans, and there is evidence that this is very important for teachers' wellbeing (Sadick and Issa 2017) and pupils' academic performance (Goodman et al. 2018; Haverinen-Shaughnessy et al. 2015). More recently, research confirmed that children (especially boys) prefer cooler temperatures than adults (Roaf, Brotas, and Nicol 2015; Teli, James, and Jentsch 2013), which is important as standards are currently generally written based on parameters for adults.
- Good acoustics and the conditions that allow clear communications to take place are intuitively important. External noise (such as traffic, airplanes, and other children playing nearby) appears to be a real problem that negatively affects academic progress (Lukas et al. 1981), but there is less evidence that internal acoustic problems in the classroom are a problem (Bluyssen 2016).

These problems can have a cumulative effect on outcomes. Glen Earthman (Earthman 2004), one of the most prolific and quoted authors on the link between basic school conditions and student achievement, has described a "poor" school as one that does not have adequate ventilation and temperature, lighting, acoustics, functional furniture, or some variation or combination of these qualities. His research has found that students in poor buildings scored between 5 and 10 percentile rank points lower than students in functional buildings on academic tests after controlling for socioeconomic status. Similarly, for higher education, there is recent evidence that indicates that test results are negatively affected where students are "outside their comfort zone" (OCZ) in relation to light, AQ, and temperature (Marchand et al. 2014).

The next section will present evidence from studies that have explored the collective impact of several elements to bridge the gulf between the high level of confidence in the literature about the different elements and a lack of extensive evidence concerning their combined effects in practice.

EVIDENCE OF HOLISTIC IMPACT OF SCHOOL SPACES ON LEARNING

Some researchers have taken a holistic approach to studying the effects of school buildings on the academic outcomes of their students by assessing the characteristics of schools as a whole (Tanner 2009). This approach has yielded insights but cannot control for individual pupil and teacher effects (which are thought to account for around 50 percent and 30 percent of pupil progress respectively (Hattie 2008; Nye, Konstantopoulos, and Hedges 2004). or fully distinguish among the various different elements of the schools being studied. Multi-level modeling may be a possible solution to this problem (US National Research Council 2006). Another issue with this approach in many cases is the reliance on the subjective views of users. While important, these views cannot be assumed to reflect what is functionally optimal (Sadick and Issa 2017), or even the observable choices that users actually make in practice (Weinstein 1982).

The Heschong Mahone Group's groundbreaking work is very revealing in this area. Their first study in 1999 (Heschong Mahone Group 1999) found a strong positive connection between high natural light levels and learning rates. However, these were not replicated when the exercise was repeated (Heschong Mahone Group 2003) in another part of the US that had hotter, drier climatic conditions. This led the Heschong Mahone researchers to make extensive further investigations, which highlighted that, in this location, views from windows were a positive influence, but glare and overheating were negative factors. They also found other confounding factors such as acoustic reverberation problems exacerbated by the variable availability of break-out spaces for one-to-one sessions. The reverberation may occur due to the open areas that have no acoustic planning or isolation materials (special ceiling, carpeting, or wall panels). Many other complex interactions between various factors were observed, for example, teachers opening windows to cool the classroom, which let in noise from adjacent sources and caused atmospheric AQ problems. What this study very clearly highlighted was the need to consider as many of the factors that affect classrooms at the same time as possible.

The Holistic Evidence and Design (HEAD) Project[2] took an unusually broad view in terms of the factors that it considered but focused in depth on a particular sort of school, namely primary schools in England. Although three geographical locations were included, the climatic conditions are all rather temperate by world standards so the results have to be interpreted accordingly. The study had the following design features:

- It factored in as wide a range of factors as possible within a new neuroscience-informed conceptual model to avoid the problem of hidden confounding factors implicit in any partial analysis.
- It addressed the issue of inadequate granularity by using multi-level modeling at the individual pupil level, the classroom level, and the whole school level.
- It went beyond students' subjective preferences by exploring the connection between the characteristics of physical school design and nationally recognized teacher assessments of pupils' academic progress—the core educational measure in the UK.
- It assessed the actual characteristics of real schools to generate practical findings relevant to the existing building stock as well as to new designs.

The starting point was the simple notion that users experience the particular spaces of their built environment via multiple sensory inputs. Examining the combined effects of these sensory inputs at the level of individual users of buildings can show how the environmental factors influence academic progress and other "emergent properties." (Checkland 1993) The implication of this approach is that the environmental factors to be studied can be selected based on not just their inherent measurability, but also on the broad structure of how the brain functions.

Drawing from Roll's (Rolls 2007) detailed description of the brain's implicit systems, the HEAD project team developed a novel organizing Environment-Behavior (E-B) model (Barrett and Barrett 2010) that reflected humans' "hard-wired" response to the availability of healthy, natural elements in their environments, their desire to be able to interact with spaces according to our individual preferences, and the various levels of visual stimulation appropriate to users engaged in different activities. Further, the team distinguished three broad categories of design elements:

- *Naturalness*: light, sound, temperature, AQ, and links to nature.
- *Individualization*: ownership, flexibility, and connection.
- *Stimulation:* visual complexity and color.

Within this structure, the team extensively researched the full range of factors (such as light and layout) that might be elements of a "good" design for schools. They studied 144 detailed papers from the literature, which yielded a clear and balanced set of factors and propositions to be tested (Barrett and Zhang 2009). The findings of the studies that provided empirical evidence of an impact on learning are briefly summarized here according to the three design categories mentioned above.

- In the *naturalness* category (which encompasses the "big four" elements—light, sound, temperature, AQ, and links to nature), much research has been carried out about optimum lighting levels (Heschong Mahone Group 1999, 2003), optimum acoustics (Canning and James 2012; Shield and Dockrell 2003), optimum learning temperatures (Szokolay 2003), and optimum AQ levels (Bakó-Biró et al. 2012; Mumovic et al. 2009). It is easy to see how each of these fundamental environmental measures could affect the ability of a child to concentrate and learn in a classroom. We included a *links to nature* element as this has been shown to improve cognitive function (Kaplan and Kaplan 1989; Tanner 2009; Wells and Evans 2003).
- Within the *individualization* category, the elements of *ownership* and *flexibility* address how well the classroom is adapted to the child's needs. *Ownership* in particular is related to how much the room is organized for both the class as a whole and for each pupil, with the aim of creating a child-centered environment that has been shown to facilitate for learning (Killeen, Evans, and Danko 2003; Skinner, Wellborn, and Connell 1990). Both *ownership* and *flexibility* have been highlighted (Higgins et al. 2005) in the research as being important aspects of the physical environment of the classroom. *Connection* is the third *individualization* parameter. It is a measure of the width and direction of corridors to make it easy to navigate around the school (Alexander, Ishikawa, and Silverstein 1977; Tanner 2009).
- The third principle of *stimulation* represents the degree of visual stimulation within a classroom. This was measured in terms of *color* and *complexity*. The scientific research into color is extensive and has shown that color can affect children's moods, mental clarity, and energy levels (Engelbrecht 2003). The measure of complexity here relates to the visual impact of both architectural and display elements in the classroom. For example, a 2014 study (Fisher, Godwin, and Seltman 2014) found more distraction and off-task behavior in children in more visually complex environments.

It can be seen that all of these factors are likely to have an effect on how well pupils learn. However, the utility of this approach depends on whether it is possible to discover the actual impact of these factors when all are experienced together.

Thus, the HEAD study (Barrett et al. 2015) made detailed assessments of 153 classrooms in 27 primary schools in three UK regions in order to identify the impact of the physical classroom features on the academic progress of the 3,766 pupils who occupied those classrooms. As can be seen, this was a big study. As primary school children spend most of their time in one classroom over a whole year, if the design of that space had any impact on their learning, then it could be expected to be detectable. The assessments recorded the particular classroom occupied by each pupil along with their starting and finishing scores in the core subjects of reading, writing, and mathematics. This meant that multi-level statistical modeling could be used to separate out the effects driven by the individual pupils' characteristics and those related to the classroom characteristics. Also, the measures of the physical characteristics of the classrooms could be isolated from broader factors at the classroom level such as teacher quality.

The HEAD study confirmed that variations in the physical design aspects of their learning environments explained 16 percent of the variation in the learning progress made by the 3,766 pupils over one year and averaged across the three subjects. This is a very significant scale of impact.

Just under a half of this percentage was due to the *naturalness* factors, with *individualization* and *stimulation* accounting for roughly one-quarter each. It is notable that the last two groups of factors, which are rarely measured, when taken together are as important as the naturalness factors.

It is interesting that all of the factors considered in the study were significant under bivariate statistical analysis with learning progress. However, the multi-level statistical modeling revealed something of the competition between factors as they interact in the real world. Once pupil effects had been controlled for, only seven key design parameters were identified: *light, temperature, AQ, ownership, flexibility, visual complexity,* and *color*. The proportions that each design parameter contributed to variations in learning progress across the sample of UK schools are shown in figure 4.1, all of which made a statistically significant difference.

FIGURE 4.1

Contribution of each classroom measure

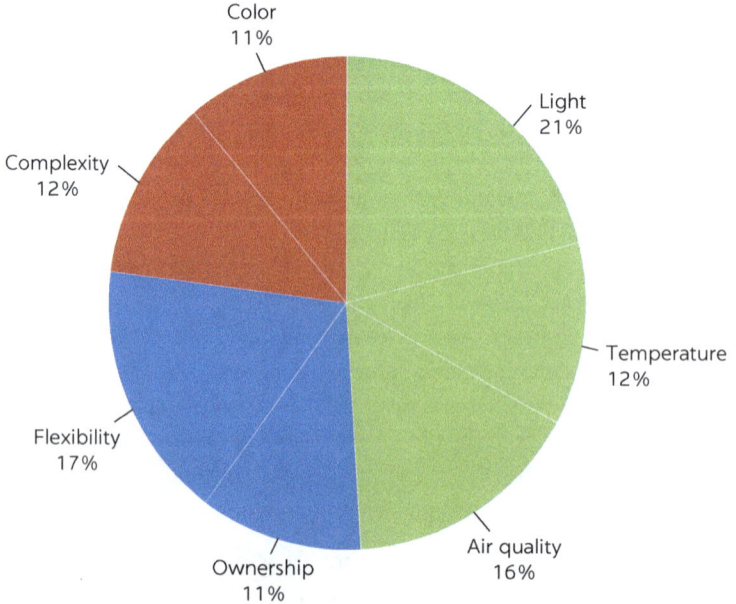

Source: Barrett et al. 2015.

These findings are a ringing endorsement of the importance of the physical design of schools not just for students' health but also to actively support their learning. The findings reinforce the notion that the impact on learning is driven by students' multidimensional experience of classroom spaces, which means that the planning process will need to carefully consider the solutions for maximizing the combined beneficial effect of these factors. It is noteworthy that the impact of these factors is even greater on children with special educational needs (SEN).

What the HEAD study did *not* find to be significant in the UK context must also be considered. Surprisingly, *acoustics* did not emerge as a significant influence. This was almost certainly because the conditions in the sample did not vary very much and were generally adequate, with classrooms being not too big and fitted with carpets and acoustic ceiling tiles. Of course, if the acoustics in a classroom were very poor, either owing to the room's design or adjacent sources of noise, then this would clearly have a very negative impact on the educational process (Canning and James 2012). *Links to nature* did not emerge as significant either initially, but after the data were reanalyzed by subject (Barrett et al. 2016), they did emerge as important, especially for writing, which requires individual creativity. For example, a 2015 study (Benfield et al. 2015) found that students in classrooms with natural views scored higher on a college writing course than those in an otherwise equivalent windowless room. Natural outdoor spaces have also been found to foster more creative play (Campbell and Frost 1985; O'Brien and Murray 2005). *Connection* did not figure in the overall analysis either, probably owing to the study's focus on pupils who used a single classroom for all subjects, but after the reanalysis by subject, it became significant for reading specifically. On further investigation, it became clear that this was related to the presence of "corridor libraries," the accessibility of which seems to have been especially beneficial for disadvantaged children in the sample. Having said that, it seems likely that the connection spaces would have more of an impact in secondary schools and universities where students circulate between different classrooms.

The final very big elements that did *not* emerge as significant were all of the school-level factors, such as outside play facilities, the external appearance and layout of the school, or even a shared ethos. This was initially very surprising, but on further consideration it became apparent that it was a consequence of a higher level of variation *within* schools in terms of the learning effectiveness of the classrooms than *between* schools. The conclusion is that any analysis aimed at designing a new school or improving an old one needs to examine each classroom in the first place. This is an argument for "inside-out design." (Frank and Lepora 2007)

Table 4.2 lists the characteristics of classroom that have been shown to improve student learning. The information presented in table 4.2 is based on the significant weight of evidence reviewed in this report and takes into account the fact that the importance of each factor will vary depending on the context.

There is solid evidence that the features highlighted above have a positive impact on learning progress. The HEAD study revealed the scale of this combined impact. As these factors are all focused on human-centric effects, they can be expected to translate well to other educational situations around the world, albeit with appropriate adjustments for differences in geography and culture. For example, plentiful fresh air, the right amount of natural light, an appropriate degree of visual stimulation, and a sense of ownership are all likely to be consistently important, but how they are achieved and which factors have most impact will vary depending on the local climatic and cultural circumstances.

TABLE 4.2 **Classroom characteristics that increase pupils' ability to learn**

DESIGN PRINCIPLE	DESIGN PARAMETER	SPECIFIC CLASSROOM FEATURES THAT IMPROVE ACADEMIC OUTCOMES
Naturalness	Light	Abundant daylight but a low risk of glare, either through orientation or shading. Also, good quality electric lighting.
	Temperature	Control of heating and cooling in each classroom. The ability to avoid heat from the sun, either through orientation or adequate external shading.
	Air quality	Big window opening sizes at different heights to provide good ventilation in varying conditions. Larger classrooms to dissipate poor air. Air conditioning where necessary.
	Acoustics	Carpeted floors and the absence of adjacent external sources of noise.
	Links to nature	Views outside and, if possible, direct access to and use of outdoor learning spaces. Natural materials in the classroom such as furniture coverings and plants.
Individualization	Ownership[a]	Distinct design characteristics, personalized displays, and high-quality chairs and desks to foster a sense of ownership among students.
	Flexibility[a]	Larger, simple areas for older children, but more varied layouts for younger pupils. Easy access to attached break-out spaces and widened corridors for pupils' storage. Well-defined learning zones that facilitate age-appropriate learning options, plus a big wall area for display.
	Connection	Wide corridors with external views where possible, plus distinctive, orientating features, especially in relation to the doorways of particular classrooms. Circulation spaces large enough to use for educational activities, such as "corridor libraries."
Stimulation	Visual Complexity[a]	Visual variety in the room layout, ceiling, and display in balance with the use of displays to create interest but with a degree of order.
	Color[a]	Light walls generally, but with a feature wall or areas highlighted with brighter color, to produce an optimal level of stimulation. Bright color on furniture and in displays as accents to the overall environment.

a. Classroom features that are strongly related to their use.

SUMMARY

There is strong evidence that the following factors all positively affect pupils' academic outcomes:

- Good "natural" conditions such as lighting, AQ, temperature control, acoustics, and links to nature
- Age-appropriate learning spaces that offer flexible learning opportunities that pupils can adapt and personalize
- Connections between learning spaces that are easy to navigate and that may provide additional learning opportunities
- Mid-level ambient stimulation using color and visual complexity
- Schools that are designed from the inside out (classroom to school) so that each space meets the needs of its inhabitants
- Designs that take into account local climatic and cultural conditions.

Educational establishments are often designed to impress, but factors that foster or impede students' capacity to learn are much more important. It makes intuitive sense that an optimal physical environment for learning should not be uncomfortable, alienating, and either chaotic or boring.

What the evidence shows is that many of the factors that affect whether an environment is healthy (as discussed in the previous section) also have a significant impact on learning. However, so do additional factors such as choices about decoration, furniture, and fittings and about how the spaces are "dressed" and used. Further, these findings indicate that there is significant potential for many existing schools to be upgraded efficiently and for new schools to be designed in ways that facilitate the learning imperative.

NOTES

1. Indoor environmental quality (IEQ) refers to the quality of a building's environment in relation to the health and wellbeing of those who occupy space within it. IEQ is determined by many factors, including lighting, air quality, and damp conditions.
2. The HEAD project was carried out by a team led by Peter Barrett, so this author must declare an interest. However, the seminal nature of the work is evidenced by the fact that the publication of the pilot results in 2013 in a leading international scientific journal led to it being the most downloaded paper that year in *Building and Environment* and to its selection as Best Paper for this journal in 2013 (with two others out of 1,300 submitted). The 2015 final results quoted here are based on five times as much data and extensive further analyses as the earlier findings.

REFERENCES

Alexander. C., S. Ishikawa, and M. Silverstein. 1977. *A Pattern Language*. New York: Oxford University Press.

Bakó-Biró, Z., D., J. Clements-Croome, N. Kochhar, H. B. Awbi, and M. J. Williams. 2012. "Ventilation Rates in Schools and Pupils' Performance." *Building and Environment* 48 (0): 215–23.

Barkmann Wessolowski, N., and M. Schulte-Markwort. 2012. "Applicability and Efficacy of Variable Light in Schools." *Physiology & Behavior* 105: 621–27.

Barrett, P., and L. Barrett. 2010. "The Potential of Positive Places: Senses, Brain and Spaces." *Intelligent Buildings International* 2: 218–28.

Barrett, P., F. Davies, Y. Zhang, and L. Barrett. 2016. "The Holistic Impact of Classroom Spaces on Learning in Specific Subjects." *Environment and Behavior* 2016.

Barrett, P. S., and L. C. Barrett. 2003. "Research as a Kaleidoscope on Practice." *Construction Management and Economics* 21: 755–66.

Barrett, P. S., F. Davies, Y. Zhang, and L. Barrett. 2015. "The Impact of Classroom Design on Pupils' Learning: Final Results of a Holistic, Multi-Level Analysis." *Building and Environment* 89: 118–33.

Barrett, P. S., and Y. Zhang. 2009. *Optimal Learning Spaces: Design Implications for Primary Schools*. Salford, UK: SCRI.

Benfield, J. A., G. N. Rainbolt, P. A. Bell, and G. H. Donovan. 2015. "Classrooms with Nature Views: Evidence of Differing Student Perceptions and Behaviors." *Environment and Behavior* 47: 140–57.

Blackmore, J., D. Bateman, J. Loughlin, J. O'Mara, and G. Aranda. 2011. *Research into the connection between built learning spaces and student outcomes*, Education, Policy and Research Division, Department of Education and Early Childhood Development, State of Victoria: Melbourne.

Bluyssen, P. M. 2016. "Health, comfort, and performance of children in classrooms: New directions for research." *Indoor and Built Environment*. Vol 26, Issue 8, 2017.

Campbell, S. D., and J. L. Frost. 1985. "The Effects of Playground Type on the Cognitive and Social Play Behaviors of Grade Two Children." In *When Children Play*, edited by J. L. Frost and S. Sunderlin, 115–20, Wheaton, MD: Association for Childhood Education International.

Canning, D., and A. James. 2012. *The Essex Study: Optimised Classroom Acoustics for All*. St Albans: The Association of Noise Consultants.

Checkland, P. 1993. *Systems Thinking, Systems Practice*. Chichester: John Wiley and Sons Ltd.

Davies, D., D. Jindal-Snape, C. Collier, and R. Digby. 2013. "Creative Learning Environments in Education: A Systematic Literature Review." *Thinking Skills and Creativity*, 8: 80–91.

Earthman, G. 2004. *Prioritization of 31 Criteria for School Building Adequacy*. Baltimore, MD: ACLU.

Engelbrecht, K. 2003. *The Impact of Color on Learning*. Chicago, IL: Perkins and Will.

Fisher, A., K. Godwin, and H. Seltman. 2014. "Visual Environment, Attention Allocation, and Learning in Young Children: When too Much of a Good Thing May Be Bad." *Psychological Science* 25: 1362–70.

Frank, K. A., and R. B. Lepora. 2007. *Architecture from the Inside Out*. 2nd ed. Hoboken, NJ: John Wiley.

Goodman, J., M. Hurwitz, J. Park, and J. Smith. 2018. "Heat and Learning." NBER Working Paper 24639.

Hattie, J. 2008. *Visible Learning: A Synthesis of over 800 Meta-Analyses Relating to Achievement*. Abingdon, UK: Routledge.

Haverinen-Shaughnessy, U., R. Shaughnessy, E. C. Cole, O. Toyinbo, and D. J. Moschandreas. 2015. "An Assessment of Indoor Environmental Quality in Schools and Its Association with Health and Performance." *Building and Environment* 93: 35–40.

Heschong Mahone Group. 1999. *Daylighting in Schools*. Fair Oaks, CA: Pacific Gas and Electric Company.

———. 2003. *Windows and Classrooms: A Study of Student Performance and the Indoor Environment*. Fair Oaks, CA: Californian Energy Commission.

Higgins, S., E. Hall, K. Wall, P. Woolner, and C. McCaughey. 2005. *The Impact of School Environments: A Literature Review*. London: Design Council.

Hopland, A., and O. Nyhus. 2015. "Does Student Satisfaction with School Facilities Affect Exam Results?" *Facilities* 33 (13/14): 760–74.

Kaplan, R., and S. Kaplan. 1989. *The Experience of Nature: A Psychological Perspective*. Cambridge: CUP.

Killeen, J., G. Evans, and S. Danko. 2003. "The Role of Permanent Student Artwork in Students' Sense of Ownership in an Elementary School." *Environment and Behavior* 35 (2): 250–63.

Kim, J., and R. de Dear. 2012. "Nonlinear Relationships between Individual IEQ Factors and Overall Workspace Satisfaction." *Building and Environment* 49: 33–44.

Lukas, J. S., R. B. DuPree, J. W. Swing. 1981. *Effects of Noise on Academic Achievement and Classroom Behavior*. Report No. FHWA/CA/DOHS-81/01. Berkley, CA: California Department of Health Services.

Marchand, G. C., N. M. Nardi, D. Reynolds, and S. Pamoukov. 2014. "The Impact of Classroom Built Environment on Student Perceptions and Learning." *Journal of Environmental Psychology* 40: 187–97.

Mumovic, P. J., M. Davies Orme, I. Ridley, T. Oreszczyn, C. Judd, H. Medina, G. Pilmoor, C. Pearson, R. Critchlow, and P. Way. 2009. "Winter Indoor Air Quality, Thermal Comfort and Acoustic Performance of Newly Built Schools in England." *Building and Environment* 44 (7): 1466–77.

Nye, B., S. Konstantopoulos, and L. Hedges. 2004. "How Large Are Teacher Effects?" *Educational Evaluation and Policy Analysis* 26 (3): 237–57.

O'Brien, L., and R. Murray. 2005. "Forest Schools in England and Wales: Woodland Space to Learn and Grow." *Environmental Education* 80: 25–27.

Roaf, S., L. Brotas, and F. Nicol. 2015. "Counting the Cost of Comfort." *Building Research & Information* 43 (3): 269–73.

Rolls, E. T. 2007. *Emotion Explained*. Oxford: Oxford University Press.

Sadick, A.-M., and M. H. Issa. 2017. "Occupants' Indoor Environmental Quality Satisfaction Factors as Measures of Teachers' Well-Being." *Building and Environment* 119: 99–109.

Schneider M. 2002. *Do School Facilities Affect Academic Outcomes?* Educational Resources Information Center, United States Department of Education, Washington, DC.

Shaughnessy, R. J., U. Haverinen-Shaughnessy, A. Nevalainen, and D. Moschandreas. 2006. "A Preliminary Study on the Association between Ventilation Rates in Classrooms and Student Performance," *Indoor Air*, 16 (6): 465–468.

Shield, B., and J. Dockrell. 2003. "The Effects of Noise on Children at School." *Building Acoustics* 10 (2): 97–116.

Skinner. E. A., J. G. Wellborn, and J. P. Connell. 1990. "What It Takes to Do Well in School and Whether I've Got It: A Process Model of Perceived Control and Children's Engagement and Achievement in School." *Journal of Educational Psychology* 82 (1): 22–32.

Szokolay, S. K. 2003. *Introduction to Architectural Science: The Basis of Sustainable Design.* Oxford: Architectural.

Tanner, C. K. 2009. "Effects of School Design on Student Outcomes." *Journal of Educational Administration* 47 (3): 381–99.

Teli, D., P. A. B. James, and M. F. Jentsch. 2013. "Thermal Comfort in Naturally Ventilated Primary School Classrooms." *Building Research & Information* 41 (3): 301–16.

Toftum, J., B. Kjeldsen, P. Wargocki, H. Mena, E. Hansen, and G. Clausen. 2015. "Association between Classroom Ventilation Mode and Learning Outcome in Danish Schools." *Building and Environment* 92: 494–503.

Toyinbo, O., R. Shaughnessy, M. Turunen, T. Putus, J. Metsamuuronen, J. Kurnitski, et al. 2016. "Building Characteristics, Indoor Environmental Quality, and Mathematics Achievement in Finnish Elementary Schools." *Building and Environment* 104: 114–21.

UNESCO Institute for Statistics. 2012. *A Place to Learn: Lessons from Research on Learning Environments*, UNESCO: Montreal.

US National Research Council. 2006. *Green Schools: Attributes for Health and Learning.* Committee to Review and Assess the Health and Productivity Benefits of Green Schools. Washington, DC: The National Academies Press.

Wargocki, P. and D. Wyon. 2007. The Effect of Moderately Raised Classroom Temperatures and Classroom Ventilation rate on the Performance of Schoolwork by Children," *HVAC&R Research* 13 (2): 193–220.

Weinstein, C. 1982. "Privacy-Seeking Behaviour in an Elementary Classroom." *Journal of Environmental Psychology* 2.

Wells, N., and G. Evans. 2003. "Nearby Nature: A Buffer of Life Stress among Rural Children." *Environment and Behavior* 35 (3): 311–30.

Wessolowski, N., H. Koenig, M. Schulte-Markwort, and C. Barkmann. 2014. "The Effect of Variable Light on the Fidgetiness and Social Behavior of Pupils in School." *Journal of Environmental Psychology* 39: 101–08.

Woolner, P., E. Hall, S. Higgins, C. McCaughey, and K. Wall. 2007. "A Sound Foundation? What We Know about the Impact of Environments on Learning and the Implications for Building Schools for the Future." *Oxford Review of Education* 33 (1): 47–70.

5 Links between School Design and Pedagogy and Community

INTRODUCTION

It is important that schools should be safe and healthy and optimally designed to be conducive to learning. However, other key factors that determine how well students learn are their interactions with their teachers mediated by the pedagogy being used. In this section, we discuss the implications of pedagogy for school layout and design. We will also discuss how schools can be designed to foster productive relationships between schools and their local communities.

PEDAGOGY AND SPACE

In many schools around the world, children are still being taught in a traditional way using didactic pedagogy. Teachers are at the front of the classroom and pupils are seated in rows facing them. This is how many teachers have been taught to teach and it can be an effective way to transmit facts.

Towards the other extreme, a 2013 OECD study of innovative learning environments (ILE) (OECD 2013) was based on seven principles that ideally should guide these learning environments (Dumont, Istance, and Benavides 2010):

- Recognizing learners as the core participants, encouraging their active engagement, and developing in them an understanding of their own activity as learners ("self-regulation")
- Being founded on the social nature of learning and actively encouraging group work and well-organized co-operative learning
- Employing learning professionals who are highly attuned to learners' motivations and the key role played by emotions in achievement
- Being acutely sensitive to individual differences among the learners, including the type and extent of their prior knowledge
- Devising programs that demand hard work and that challenge everyone without excessive overloading them

- Operating with clarity of expectations and using assessment strategies consistent with these expectations, with a strong emphasis on formative feedback to support learning
- Strongly promoting "horizontal connectedness" across areas of knowledge and subjects as well as with the community and the wider world.

Between and beyond these positions are a wide range of theoretical frameworks and models concerning the nature of and influences on learning. For example, in 2012, UNESCO (UNESCO Institute for Statistics 2012) reviewed nine perspectives that range in their assumptions about how learning takes place and the conditions that are conducive to it.

So, in practical terms pedagogies can be seen to stretch from a purely didactic model, through blended approaches (as observed in almost all of the UK HEAD primary school sample, for example), to highly pupil-centric learning models. The blended approach typically involves islands of tables with four to six children together with a range of learning zones (Barrett et al. 2015), such as a reading corner and a wet area. This approach supports occasional teaching from the front, but more normally, enabling children to work in groups or pairs and to self-direct activities in a learning zone as well as one-on-one interventions by the teacher. Clearly, these different approaches require different space configurations (Guney and Selda 2012), and this has been clearly illustrated in Russian Federation (Shmis, Kotnik, and Ustinova 2014) where a distinction is made between "institutional typologies" reflecting didactic approaches and more open and flexible "educational landscapes" to support more complex, child-centered pedagogies.

It would seem fair to argue that there is a global trend towards a pupil-centric view, which is in keeping with notion of "zones of proximal development" as expounded by Lev Vygotsky, the Soviet developmental psychologist (Vygotsky 1978). In this approach, it can be argued that the teacher, the spaces, and the pedagogy (see figure 5.1) can all help the pupil to go beyond their current developmental stage and reach a higher skill level.

This resonates with the OECD ILE principles, which consider the learning environment as a much broader concept than just the physical environment. This was also reflected in a 2005 literature review (Higgins et al. 2005), which concluded that the impact of changes in the physical environment on cognitive and affective measures must be based on an understanding of the complexity of the many interacting pedagogical, socio-cultural, curricular, motivational, and socioeconomic factors that operate in schools. Clearly this is not a simple matter of architectural determinism.

The most obvious aspect of the relationship between pedagogy and space is layout, in particular cellular classrooms versus flexible or open configurations. This is a complex issue (Blackmore et al. 2011), which has been explored in several studies that were not conclusive about the impact of flexibility on pupils' achievements nor about the value of either open plan or cellular layouts (Deed and Lesko 2015; Saltmarsh et al. 2015; Stone 2001). However, a study (Scott-Webber et al. 2013) was recently conducted in four US universities using an instrument called Active Learning Post Occupancy Evaluation Tool. The majority of students surveyed rated non-traditional classroom design better on each of 12 factors, which included collaboration, active involvement, the ability to use the most effective learning methods (as specified in the survey), physical movement, and the creation of an enriching experience. The Reggio Emilia[1] concept points to the learning environment as a "third teacher," because if the best

FIGURE 5.1
Learning interactions: Teacher, spaces, and pedagogy

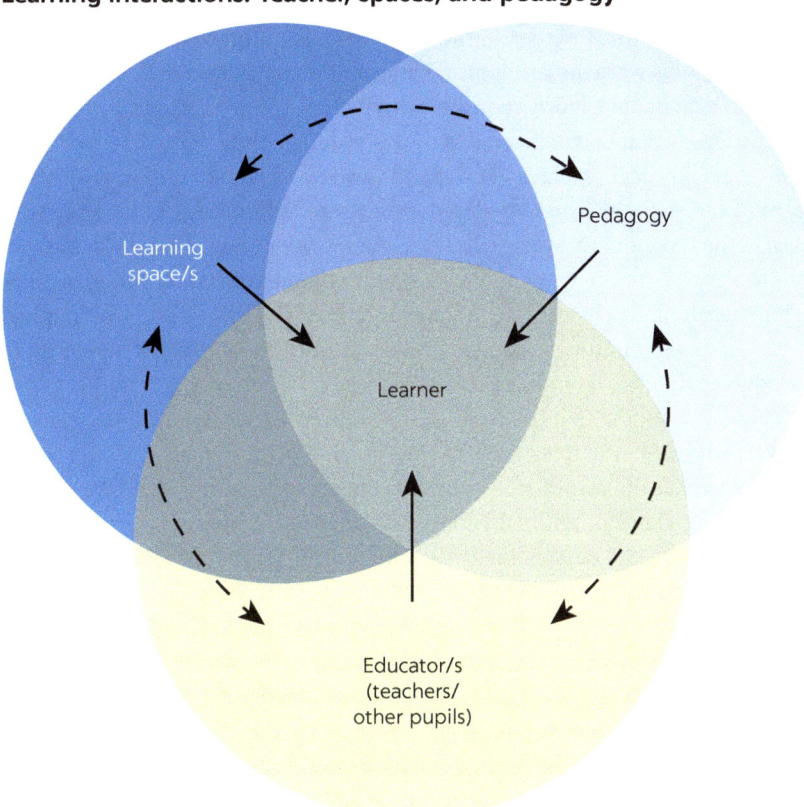

Source: Barrett et al. 2015.

learning environment is populated with poorly trained teachers, broken interactions between students, a weak curriculum, and a loose management system, this will not result in good learning. The learning environment works as a third teacher only after the teacher-learner and learner-learners interactions.

On the other hand, some teachers have argued that open spaces are actually not as flexible for teaching and learning as traditional classrooms and associated cellular spaces that together allow for discrete activities to be carried out simultaneously (Zhang and Barrett 2010). In either case, the question of structure in the class has to be answered for each school and has to be subject of the educational policy (Deed and Lesko 2015). In Norway (Barrett and Barrett 2016), the creation of flexible spaces has had unintended consequences in that they have been found to create a low level of stimulation and a situation where no one feels any ownership of an particular space.

This is a clearly a greatly contested area. Recent longitudinal case study reviews (Daniels 2015; Daniels et al. 2017) have detailed the experience of four schools that were built as part of the UK Building Schools for the Future (BSF) program in 2003–10 plus one school that missed out on funding and so remained in its old buildings. The new BSF secondary schools were aspirational and tended to be built based on open designs, driven by head teachers with a strong vision and the goal of implementing a flexible, student-centered pedagogy. These longitudinal studies threw light on the mixed results of this experiment and the reasons behind them.

One school was, and is, an ongoing success story. The head teacher had acted as the client, had remained in post, and had worked very hard with and supported all staff on the new pedagogical approach. This approach was consonant with and to some extent driven by the spaces provided and resulted in good outcomes all round. However, in the other schools, various problems occurred. These problems were the result of staff not sharing the educational vision or the head teacher changing fairly soon after completion of the building and introducing a pedagogy that was not suited to the open design of the school. In two cases, significant physical changes were made (walls were built) within only a few years of the school being completed in order to create more cellular spaces. Clearly, the BSF initiative was devised to promote a certain kind of pedagogy and thus the infrastructure was built in such a way that there was no way to go back to how teaching had been done previously. Conversely, the one school that had to stay in its old buildings was fatally hampered by the buildings' structure in introducing the new approach to teaching.

These cases show that the main goal should be to ensure an appropriate fit between the spaces in question and the evolving pedagogy used within them. However, given the turbulence caused by changing head teachers and diverse and evolving views of optimal pedagogies relative to the long-term nature of school buildings, the implication is clear that flexibility for users should be built in from the start. Because change is occurring in the area of pedagogy, there is value in thinking in terms of Vygotsky's (Vygotsky 1978) notion of "zones of proximal development" in relation to the teachers themselves, who will need support to change along with the pedagogy and spaces, especially if they are expected to be advocates for, and drivers of, that change.

The results of the case studies also highlighted the distinction between "open" and "flexible," which too often are rolled into a single composite phrase. Atkin (2011) put it powerfully when she called for the debate to: "move beyond the simplicity of flexible open spaces to integrate resource rich, special purpose spaces with flexible, adaptable multipurpose spaces to provide a dynamic workshop environment for learning." The effectiveness of openness depends fundamentally on the level at which it is applied. For example, a large cellular classroom with many learning zones may have walls, but it has the potential to be very flexible. This flexibility is quite commonly enhanced by the use of folding (soundproofed) walls, thus allowing spaces to be used together or separately in different configurations. These could also be used in closely related spaces as Atkin argues for, or the "openness" could apply throughout the school. As Rogic (2014) put it: "ultimately the ideal learning space will be different for every school depending on the school's pedagogical vision and its context."

These issues are not only relevant to new schools. Changes in classroom design, furniture selection, and layout can be introduced in existing buildings as well.

IMPROVING SCHOOLS AND INCREASING COMMUNITY WELLBEING

It is common for education experts to call for schools to engage with their surrounding communities. For example, this was one of the selection criteria for the OECD's "exemplary schools." (OECD CELE 2011) Community engagement is a multifaceted issue. It can consist of intensive use of the school's physical facilities by the broader community and/or the extension of pupils' learning into the wider community, not only in terms of what and where they learn but also in terms of pupils acting as teachers within the community. By playing such an ambassadorial role, the students would be emphasizing the school as a symbol for the value placed on education. In advanced, urban societies, the norm is for the community to use the school facilities, but in remote rural communities where economic development is greatly needed, then the extension of education and skills into the community is tremendously valuable.

Education does not happen in a vacuum. School buildings are deeply rooted in the communities that they serve, and both pupils and teachers interact with the social and built environment around each school. In most communities, school buildings are the most prominent public building, the center of many civic activities, social life, and sports events, in addition to cultural and educational activities. Also, in many cases, school buildings are the largest capital asset in a residential neighborhood. In an Economic Policy Institute Briefing in 2008, Mary Filardo (Filardo 2008)—Executive Director, 21st Century School Fund, pointed out that the key to the economic prosperity of American communities and the US nation used to be the public schools. Filardo noted that responsible management of and investment in school buildings pays off in three ways: in skilled jobs in local communities, in the quality of life that healthy, safe, and educationally appropriate buildings create for students and teachers, and in the benefits that quality education yields for generations to come.

Schools often have facilities such as large halls and sports grounds and equipment that the local community may otherwise lack. Providing community members with access to these facilities can yield many benefits (Seydel 2017). Though it may sometimes create some security complications, these can usually be resolved by allowing adults to use the facility only after normal school hours. This can also be a source of additional income for many schools in developed nations.

As mentioned above, the school's involvement with the community can also mean providing students with educational opportunities outside the school. Learning can take place in an informal way pretty much anywhere (Gehl 2011). On the way to school, in a street, at the local library, at a neighborhood theater, at the coffee table of the central plaza, or even at a canteen or a hospital given the right circumstances. All kind of resources can be used creatively to do this, including communications technology. Especially when there are space constraints, taking students beyond out of the school boundaries can be a very enriching experience. This can extend to learning from elders in the community, for example, to create living history projects.

More than a century ago Maria Montessori (Montessori 2013) stressed the importance of the senses in the learning process. When a school building looks ugly, dirty, and in a depleted natural environment, with broken glass and falling plaster, students learn the diminished value that their institutions place on them and their future. This bleak scenario is aggravated when other schools not far away look much better, which can fuel social resentment. The British Commission for Architecture and the Built Environment[2] named "identity and context" as the top criterion for successful school design. The Commission explained that it is very important to "make a school of which students and community can be proud." They emphasized that a successful school construction or renovation project has to embody the ethos and identity of a school, to contribute to the neighborhood beyond its site boundaries, and establish the school as an attractive presence in the community.

The effects of an attractive school facility reach much further than the pupils themselves. Imagine relatively uneducated parents seeing their children being educated in good quality school buildings, having access to exciting educational resources, and, in some cases, gaining more skills and knowledge than the parents themselves. If parents feel that the attractive school environment gives them opportunities as well, then this will increase the development impact of the school on the community as a whole. This can be done by giving parents and other community members access to the schools' resources, such as computers or language materials, perhaps along with some basic tuition. It can also involve older people being inspired so that the children themselves can help them gain educational traction. Why should the peer-to-peer learning ("second teacher") take place only in school buildings? A school building often is, and almost always could be, the center of community life. When schools embrace the concept of lifelong learning, this opens the reach of education to a wider range of potential users (World Bank 2003, 2011) and, at the same time, brings community members to the school and closer to decisions about what, where, and how.

Discussing the relationship between schools and communities, the architectural psychologist Rotraut Walden (Walden 2015) has argued that the key to providing school facilities that meet current and future needs in a given community is to constantly scan the environment, communicate regularly with educators, community leaders, businesses, and policymakers and to stay aware of current, educational, design, and environmental issues. Denmark has developed its own approach[3] to enabling and sustaining community engagement in school design by involving all stakeholders in the planning process. These stakeholders might include the municipal leader who is in charge of education, civil works planners and architects, the future principal and his/her deputy, school teachers, representatives of the teachers' union, the parents' association, and the board of trustees, and the community manager designated for the construction project.

SUMMARY

There is growing evidence that the best ways to ensure that the design and layout of schools support the pedagogy are:

- Striving to create innovative spaces for learning while also respecting the professionalism of the educationalists involved and their current traditions, skills, and constraints
- Creating schools that are spatially flexible so that over the long term they can support rather than obstruct any changes or developments in pedagogical practice
- Implementing any innovations in educational practice by ensuring that there is a consistent "fit" between the vision behind the innovation, teachers' capabilities and motivations, and the characteristics of the spaces that are available
- Where necessary, increasing the flexibility of *existing* schools by using new furniture and fittings as well as by investing in alterations and extensions.

There can also be many advantages to seeing the school not just as a building but in the context of its community, for instance:

- Involve community stakeholders in the planning and use of school facilities

- Explore the potential of using available community resources to help pupils to learn
- Allow community members to use the school's facilities and equipment to further their own education and improve their skills.

NOTES

1. Reggio-Emilia is a region in Italy, which became a birthplace of the Reggio-Emilia pedagogical approach developed by the Italian pedagogue Loris Malaguzzie in 1950s. To learn more, see the website http://www.reggiochildren.it/?lang=en.
2. To learn more, see the website http://webarchive.nationalarchives.gov.uk/20110118095356/ http://www.cabe.org.uk/design-review/schools/criteria.
3. See http://modelprogram.dk/.

REFERENCES

Atkin, J. 2011. *Transforming Spaces for Learning*, in OECD CELE, *Designing for Education: Compendium of Exemplary Educational Facilities 2011*. Paris: OECD.

Barrett, P. S. and L. C. Barrett. 2016. *HEAD for Norway: Knowledge Transfer Project for School Design for Learning*. Buxton, UK: Nutbox Consultancy.

Barrett, P. S., Y. Zhang, F. Davies, and L. Barrett. 2015. *Clever Classrooms: Summary Report of the HEAD Project*. Salford: University of Salford.

Blackmore, J., D. Bateman, J. Loughlin, J. O'Mara, and G. Aranda. 2011. *Research into the Connection between Built Learning Spaces and Student Outcomes*. Melbourne: Education, Policy and Research Division, Department of Education and Early Childhood Development, State of Victoria.

Daniels, H. 2015. "Continuity and Conflict in School Design: A Case Study from Building Schools for the Future." *Intelligent Buildings International* 7 (2–3): 64–82.

Daniels, H., H. M. Tse, A. Stables, and S. Cox. 2017. "Design as a Social Process: The Design of New Build Schools." *Oxford Review* 43 (6): 767–87.

Deed, C., and T. Lesko. 2015. "'Unwalling' The Classroom: Teacher Reaction and Adaptation." *Learning Environment Research* 18: 217–31.

Dumont, H., D. Istance, and F. Benavides. eds. 2010. *The Nature of Learning: Using Reseach to Inspire Practice*. Educational Research and Innovation. Paris: OECD Publishing.

Filardo, M. 2008. *Good Buildings, Better Schools: An Economic Stimulus Opportunity with Long-term Benefits*. Washington, D.C.: Economic Policy Institute. Briefing Paper #216.

Gehl, J. 2011. *Life between Buildings: Using Public Space*. Washington, DC: Island Press.

Guney, A., and A. Selda. 2012. "Effective Learning Environments in Relation to Different Learning Theories." *Procedia—Social and Behavioural Sciences* 46: 2334–38.

Higgins, S., E. Hall, K. Wall, P. Woolner, and C. McCaughey. 2005. *The Impact of School Environments: A Literature Review*. London: Design Council.

Montessori, M. 2013. *The Montessori Method*. New Brunswick, NJ: Transaction Publishers.

OECD. 2013. *Innovative Learning Environments*. Paris: Educational Research and Innovation.

OECD CELE. 2011. *Designing for Education: Compendium of Exemplary Educational Facilities 2011*. Paris: OECD Publishing.

Rogic, T. 2014. *Shaping Learning*. Perkins+Will Research Journal. Chicago, IL.

Saltmarsh, S., A. Chapman, M. Campbell, and C. Drew. 2015. "Putting 'Structure within Space': Spatially Un/Responsive Pedagogic Practices in Open-Plan Learning Environments." *Educational Review* 67 (3): 315–27.

Scott-Webber, Lennie, Aileen Stickland, and Laura Ring Kapitula. 2013. Built Environments Impact Behaviours: Results of an Active Learning Post-Occupancy Evaluation. *Planning for Higher Education Journal*. V42 N1 October-December. https://www.k12blueprint.com/sites/default/files/Built-Environments.pdf.

Seydel, O. 2017. "Reflections on the Relationship between Schools and the City." In *Education, Space, and Urban Planning*, edited by A. Million, Switzerland: Springer International Publishing.

Shmis, T., J. Kotnik, and M. Ustinova. 2014. "Creating New Learning Environments: Challenges for Eraly Childhood Development Architecture and Pedagogy in Russia." *Procedia—Social and Behavioral Sciences* 146: 40–46.

Stone, N. J. 2001. "Designing Effective Study Environments." *Journal of Environmental Psychology* 21 (2): 179–90.

UNESCO Institute for Statistics. 2012. *A Place to Learn: Lessons from Research on Learning Environments*. Montreal: UNESCO.

Vygotsky, L. 1978. *Mind in Society: Development of Higher Psychological Processes*. Boston, MA: Harvard College.

Walden, R. ed. 2015. *Schools of the Future. Design Proposals from Architectural Psychology*. Berlin: Springer.

World Bank. 2003. *Lifelong Learning in the Global Knowledge Economy: Challenges for Developing Countries*. Washington, DC: The International Bank for Reconstruction and Development.

———. 2011. *Learning for All: Investing in People's Knowledge and Skills to Promote Development*. Washington DC: The International Bank for Reconstruction and Development.

Zhang, Y., and P. Barrett. 2010. "Findings from a Post-Occupancy Evaluation in the UK Primary Schools Sector." *Facilities* 28 (13): 641–56.

6 The Process of Effective Planning and Implementation

School facilities do not just appear. They have to be created, either through the construction of new buildings or the adaptation of existing ones, and this involves many people and significant challenges. To ensure that schools have the maximum impact on the learning and development of their students, planners take into account all of the issues covered so far in this report and the implementation process needs to be characterized by dialogue, ambition, inspiration, economy, sustainability, and a long-term, holistic perspective.

THE NEED FOR DIALOGUE

The two most common objectives of educational improvement programs are to expand access to schooling and to improve its quality. Equity, completion, efficiency, purpose, and accountability are other important goals that are imbedded in the main two goals. Underlying all of these objectives is improving governance to ensure that all ideas can be implemented as planned. The attainment of each and all of these objectives can be helped or hindered by the availability, characteristics, and condition of existing educational facilities as well as the administrative and technical structures deployed to this end.

When drafting an educational improvement program, it is very important to understand the implications of the relationship between those who understand and formulate educational needs and those who can design and build the facilities to meet those needs. How one can positively influence the other and make the whole better. Of course, whether for new buildings or adaptations, for big or small projects, designers should listen to users to make sure that the ultimate infrastructure meets users' needs and purposes (Barrett and Stanley 1999).

It is also critical that educators, administrators, and facility planners develop a common language and understanding of different options and of their costs and long-term benefits. Achieving this effective communication within specific projects requires an ongoing dialogue between designers and educators, which will probably be facilitated in due course by more comprehensive research and tools that have yet to emerge (Cleveland and Fisher 2014). Many authors have stressed the importance of this dialogue throughout a lengthy and dynamic process (Cleveland and Fisher 2014; Woolner et al. 2017). It needs to be flexible enough to deal with challenges such as a change of head teacher in the middle of the project, which can often create practical problems if the new head teacher has a different vision of pedagogy (Daniels et al. 2017). Another challenge can be helping teachers to adapt to the new facilities, which has been described as "a continual process of negotiation." (Deed and Lesko 2015)

It is interesting to note that the Harvard Graduate School of Education is currently teaching a course[1] called Learning Environments for Tomorrow: Next Practices for Educators and Architects. After decades of detailed research about the relationship between student achievement and the built environment, it is refreshing to see now that a major university is committed to the value of educators and architects working together.

This dialogue is also the mechanism for considering findings from other similar projects and for digesting, reassessing, and combining them into solutions that fit the specific climate, culture, and resources (Lillrank 1995) of the project in question. The absolute necessity for this is illustrated by the findings of the excellent Heschong Mahone studies. The first study in 1999 (Heschong Mahone Group 1999) found that more daylight had a significant positive impact on learning compared with lower daylight, but their subsequent 2003 study, (Heschong Mahone Group 2003) which was conducted in an area with different climatic conditions, did not find this, but did find that other issues, such as acoustics and air quality were more influential on outcomes. This is a powerful reminder that, although we have a strong grasp of the factors that influence learning, we have to interpret these carefully in the very particular context of each project.

THE NEED FOR AMBITION

The need for clients and service providers to work together is especially necessary in the early stages of a project or program when ideas are still fresh and the physical form of the building, or adaptations to a building, have not yet been well defined. Often the process starts with a strong vision statement like: "Every school provides a world-class education…"[2] or "….the Los Angeles Unified School District believes in the equal worth and dignity of all students and is committed to educate all students to their maximum potential."[3] These are very powerful ideas that should infuse all of the decisions still to be made from the planning stage onwards to design, construction, and operations to maintenance. They should even guide curriculum updates, teacher training plans, strategies for using technology, and even the layout of furniture in classrooms as well as the relationship between the project building and the rest of the school campus where relevant.

Facility planners, architects, and engineers need to have a very clear understanding of the goals of educators in order to make specific decisions about such simple but important issues like the use of daylight, the quality of the tiles in the bathrooms, and the electrical and data distribution network. This is not always simple in practice as can be seen in this interesting example from Norway.[4] Several schools in Norway were built using public-private partnerships (PPP) and continue to be maintained by the same contractors. These schools have a clause forbidding teachers from sticking display material onto the walls, which makes maintenance easier, but fundamentally hampers the teachers in their normal practices.

Planners should also aim to improve equity in access. While access for students, teachers, and community members with disabilities is usually enshrined in the law, this does not mean that it is universally enforced, which reinforces inequity. Rural areas with low population density and difficult terrain present a particular challenge that needs to be resolved at the micro-planning level, looking specifically for an efficient operation of the whole municipal planning system (transportation, communication, and accessibility).

THE NEED FOR INSPIRATION

Many innovative and ambitious designs have been used around the world to construct or repurpose school buildings. These can be a source of inspiration for governments, clients, and designers working on their own projects. Here are some sources that discuss those inspirational designs and ideas:

- The OECD Center for Effective Learning Environments published "Designing for Education: A Compendium of Exemplary Educational Facilities" in 2011, which described 60 exemplary educational facilities that had been selected in worldwide competition (OECD CELE 2011).
- The LEED[5] certification program recognizes the importance of making the school building itself a teaching tool by recommending the integration of the sustainable features of the school facility into the school's educational mission.
- The Third Teacher Book (O'Donnel et al. 2010) offers 79 practical design ideas to improve schools.
- The Language of School Design (Nair and Fiedling 2005) offers 25 design patterns to be considered for 21st Century schools.
- The University of Melbourne prepared a review in the framework of the "Innovative Learning Environments & Teacher Change" project (ILETC),[6] which analyses different types of learning environments in Australian and New Zealand schools and how the teachers use it (Imms et al. 2017).

Additionally, there are several private and institutional initiatives that support the development of high-quality educational facilities designed to improve student outcomes:

- The Association for the Learning Environment[7]
- The International Union of Architects, Architecture, and Children Program[8]
- The Organization for Economic Co-operation and Development, Center for Effective Learning Environments[9]
- The National Clearinghouse for Educational Facilities in the US[10]
- Education Facilities Clearinghouse.[11]

All of these institutions, authors, and professionals around the world have recognized the need for safe, healthy, sustainable, and educationally sound educational facilities.

THE NEED FOR A LONG-TERM, HOLISTIC PERSPECTIVE

A pioneer document written by Arnold Oates and Lee Bruch (Oates and Burch 1999) in 1999 advocated for taking a holistic approach to the planning process in the context of scarce resources for education. The authors put great emphasis on consulting with stakeholders and ensuring that planners use well-grounded information as a basis for decision-making. This information needs to encompass demographics, socioeconomic factors, the economy, culture, technology, the political landscape, legal issues, and environmental conditions.

In 2011, in response to the proliferation of inadequate building plans that emphasized a few aspects but ignored others, Mary Filardo (Filardo 2011) wrote a master plan evaluation guide. It highlights the importance of stakeholders' participation, evidence-based decision-making, and the need for a clear vision to inspire the whole school system. Additionally, it sets out a logical order for master plans and goes into great detail about every step of the process. Even though it is meant to evaluate existing plans, it can also be used as a guide for future plans by breaking down key activities, none of which should be overlooked, rushed, or avoided.

A key strategic challenge in the mid to long term will be the volatile issue of demographic change. This is relevant to individual school projects but is even more salient for regional and national programs. Radical shifts in age profiles are occurring within the populations of many countries, and there are huge movements of people through urbanization and, more chaotically, through refugee movements across the world. In Romania, for example, despite recent school closures and consolidations, it has recently been established that 22 percent of pupils are in over-crowded classrooms and 34 percent are in under-utilized spaces.[12] Assessing these issues at a strategic level is a significant modeling challenge that depends on collecting and analyzing population data together with geospatial data using assumptions about how such issues as ethnic mix will affect the number and types of school places needed in the future. To devise plans that can accommodate these unpredictable issues within physical infrastructure that is likely to be in use for decades, it is important to build flexibility into the design. The design should take into account the need to adapt to shifts in the mix of usage (such as the age profile of students) within the existing facility, to grow the educational establishment in the future if overall demand rises, and to facilitate alternative uses for the space if demand drops. This flexibility could be as simple as leaving space on the site for future growth or designing space with alternative uses in mind.

When public or borrowed money is used to fund capital investment in school infrastructure projects, there is a strong need to account for how the funds are invested and for actually delivering the promised benefits to society. When designed and implemented correctly, the school facilities can provide benefits to society far beyond its walls for many years to come.

SUMMARY

There are four key elements that should characterize the implementation of a school infrastructure project in order to realize its full benefits:

- There should be ongoing dialogue between planners, educators, and facility designers to take advantage of their complementary areas of expertise, to build in value for the wider community, and, vitally, to take account of international evidence in the context of each particular project.

- The process should be ambitious in terms of its vision, particularly in terms of being strongly committed to achieving equality.
- Planners should take account of examples of inventive solutions developed elsewhere around the world for inspiration in resolving their particular challenges.
- Planners should take a long-term, holistic perspective to the design of the facility, particularly with regard to building in flexibility to accommodate any demographic or pedagogical changes in the decades ahead.

There are many volumes of advice on practical management techniques for school infrastructure projects, but this is not the place to review them. Instead we have focused on the characteristics of the implementation process that are necessary to deliver the full educational benefits of these projects.

NOTES

1. See https://www.gse.harvard.edu/ppe/program/learning-environments-tomorrow-next-practices-educators-and-architects.
2. District of Columbia Public Schools.
3. Los Angeles Unified School District.
4. Private correspondence with Siv Marit Stavem of Norconsult AS, 7/26/17.
5. See https://new.usgbc.org/leed for more information.
6. See http://www.iletc.com.au.
7. For more information, see http://a4le.org.
8. More information at https://www.architectureandchildren-uia.com/.
9. http://www.oecd.org/edu/innovation-education/centreforeffectivelearningenvironmentscele/.
10. See http://www.ncef.org/ for more information.
11. See http://www.efc.gwu.edu for more information.
12. Private correspondence with Janssen Edelweiss Teixeira, Senior Education Specialist at the World Bank in Washington, based on a recent study of education infrastructure in Romania.

REFERENCES

Barrett, P. S., and C. Stanley. 1999. *Better Construction Briefing*. Blackwell Science. p. 157.

Cleveland, B., and K. Fisher. 2014. "The Evaluation of Physical Learning Environments: A Critical Review of the Literature." *Learning Environments Research* 17 (1): 1–28.

Daniels, H., H. M. Tse, A. Stables, and S. Cox. 2017. "Design as a Social Process: The Design of New Build Schools." *Oxford Review* 43 (6): 767–87.

Deed, C., and T. Lesko. 2015. "'Unwalling' The Classroom: Teacher Reaction and Adaptation." *Learning Environment Research* 18: 217–31.

Filardo, M. 2011. *PK-12 Education Facilities Master Plan Evaluation Guide*. Washington, D.C.: 21st Century School Fund.

Heschong Mahone Group. 1999. *Daylighting in Schools*. Fair Oaks, CA: Pacific Gas and Electric Company.

———. 2003. *Windows and Classrooms: A Study of Student Performance and the Indoor Environment*. Fair Oaks, CA: Californian Energy Commission.

Imms, W., Mahat, M., Byers, T. & Murphy, D. 2017. Type and Use of Innovative Learning Environments in Australasian Schools ILETC Survey No. 1. Melbourne: University of Melbourne, LEaRN, Retrieved from: http://www.iletc.com.au/publications/reports.

Lillrank, P. 1995. "The Transfer of Management Innovations from Japan." *Organisational Studies* 16 (6): 971–89.

Nair, Prakash, and Randall Fiedling. 2005. *The Language of School Design*. DesignShare, Minneapolis, USA.

Oates, A. and L. Burch. 1999. *A Model Schedule for a Capital Improvement Program*. ERIC.

O'Donnell Wicklund Pigozzi and Peterson, Bruce Mau, David W. Orr. 2010. *The Third Teacher Book*, Abrams Books.

OECD CELE. 2011. *Designing for Education: Compendium of Exemplary Educational Facilities 2011*. Paris: OECD Publishing.

Woolner, P., E. Hall, S. Higgins, C. McCaughey, and K. Wall (2007). "A Sound Foundation? What We Know about the Impact of Environments on Learning and the Implications for Building Schools for the Future," *Oxford Review of Education*, 33 (1): 47–70.

7 Summary and Conclusions

SUMMARY

We have reviewed a large volume of powerful research to gather evidence of the most important aspects of school design that particularly affect pupils' academic outcomes. These aspects can be categorized in five main areas.

Access to school places

There is strong evidence that the following elements all contribute positively to pupils' academic outcomes (see Section 2):

- Relatively small schools
- Schools locally distributed to maintain reasonable travel to school distances
- Relatively small classes
- Relatively low density of classroom occupancy
- Reasonable length of school days
- Optimal scheduling of the use of spaces to maximize educational benefit.

Each country and, in some cases, each province or district have their own parameters that are used in planning. This information is typically presented in codes or standards that apply to all government-sponsored school construction. All of the particular elements described above should be discussed as part of a Facilities Master Planning process to identify challenges and to establish priorities for the allocation of funds.

Safe and healthy schools

There is strong evidence that the following factors all positively increase the chances of pupils and teachers attending school, remaining healthy at school, and, in the case of teachers, staying in their profession:

- Schools that are soundly built and proof against natural disasters
- The provision of and access to basic services, such as water, sanitation, waste disposal, electricity and communications

- Good indoor environmental quality, especially in relation to air quality and dampness
- Opportunities for outside play
- Schools that are maintained in good physical condition
- Regulations and standards that are enforced effectively on the ground
- Training that shows users how to get the maximum health and learning benefits from their school infrastructure.

These are quite basic aspirations, but the evidence shows that school buildings often fall short and that, when they do, it is often the most disadvantaged students who get the worst provision. UNESCO has found that most countries have sound regulations for school building, so the focus needs to be on the effective implementation of these standards in every country and region. This could be supplemented with initiatives to share good practices between first world countries and developing countries.

Optimal spaces for learning

There is strong evidence that the following characteristics of learning spaces all positively contribute to pupils' academic outcomes:

- Good "natural" conditions such as lighting, air quality, temperature control, acoustics, and links to nature
- Age-appropriate learning spaces that offer flexible learning opportunities that pupils can adapt and personalize
- Connections between learning spaces that are easy to navigate and that may provide additional learning opportunities
- Mid-level ambient stimulation using color and visual complexity
- Schools that are designed from the inside out (classroom to school) so that each space meets the needs of its inhabitants
- Designs that take into account local climatic and cultural conditions.

It makes intuitive sense that an optimal physical environment should not be uncomfortable, alienating, or either chaotic or boring. What the evidence shows is that many of the factors relevant for ensuring a healthy environment, covered in the previous section, also have a significant impact on learning. However, so do additional factors such as choices about decoration, furniture, and fittings and about how the spaces are "dressed" and used. Our findings indicate that there is a huge amount of potential for many existing schools to be upgraded very economically and for new schools to be designed in ways that facilitate the learning imperative.

Maximizing the benefits of pedagogy and the school-community relationship

There is growing evidence that the best ways to ensure that the design and layout of schools support pedagogy are:

- Striving to meet the OECD's Innovative Learning Environment objectives while also respecting the professionalism of the educationalists involved and their current traditions, skills, and constraints
- Creating schools that are spatially flexible so that over the long term they can support rather than obstruct any changes or developments in pedagogical practice

- Implementing any innovations in educational practice by ensuring that there is a consistent "fit" between the vision behind the innovation, teachers' capabilities and motivations, and the characteristics of the spaces that are available
- Where necessary, increasing the flexibility of *existing* schools by using new furniture and fittings as well as by investing in alterations and extensions.

Many gains can result from seeing the school not just as a building but in the context of its community. The evidence for these gains is not solid, but they are intuitively attractive. To make them more likely, it is suggested planners should:

- Involve community stakeholders in the planning and use of school facilities
- Explore the potential of using available community resources to help pupils to learn Allow community members to use the school's facilities and equipment to further their own education and improve their skills.

The process of effective planning and implementation

To ensure that schools, whether new or adapted, have the maximum impact on the learning and development of their students, planners need to take into account all of the evidence, and the implementation process should have the following characteristics:

- There should be ongoing dialogue between planners, educators, and facility designers to take advantage of their complementary areas of expertise, to build in value for the wider community, and, vitally, to take account of international evidence in the context of each particular project.
- The process should be ambitious in terms of its vision, particularly in terms of being strongly committed to achieving equality.
- Planners should take account of examples of inventive solutions developed elsewhere around the world for inspiration in resolving their particular challenges.
- Planners should take a long-term, holistic perspective to the design of the facility, particularly with regard to building in flexibility to accommodate any demographic or pedagogical changes in the decades ahead.

There are many volumes of advice on practical management techniques for school infrastructure projects, but this is not the place to review them. Instead we have focused on the characteristics of the implementation process that are necessary to deliver the full educational benefits of these projects.

IMPLICATIONS FOR FUTURE PRACTICE

Having a better shared understanding of how the design of school infrastructure affects educational outcomes is very useful for those doing education sector work. The evidence presented in this report shows that a wider range of salient factors can possibly be addressed with the right planning approach. This will make it possible to develop better projects and to meet the specific needs of the children and teachers in question, which may also improve educational outcomes. It will potentially increase the efficiency of the resources invested in school infrastructure projects and will lead to more effective cooperation between the different specialists involved in the development of school infrastructure.

IMPLICATIONS FOR FUTURE RESEARCH

The range of issues covered in this report is based on multiple sources of evidence of varying strength. There is much to build on immediately, but further research effort of various types would be valuable in the following areas:

- In relation to spaces that are optimal for learning (see section 4), there is strong evidence from studies in the developed world about what factors are critical for achieving positive learning outcomes. However, further studies are needed to explore what kinds of spaces are best for learning in different climates and cultures. It can be expected that some issues will be more or less important than others depending on local conditions.
- Cross-cultural, comparative impact evaluation studies would be valuable to explore the issue of the optimal provision of places through the choice of school disposition and size.
- The evidence for the importance of safe and healthy schools is strong, but investigations are urgently needed into how to make this happen effectively in the context of existing country regulations (UNESCO 2012).
- Case studies are showing the importance of matching the chosen pedagogy with the spaces provided, but large-scale research will be needed to confirm this, not only at a given point in time but also in transitions when teachers are having to adapt to change.
- There are persuasive arguments in favor of the contention that involving the whole range of stakeholders in all of the different stages of school planning has a positive effect on outcomes, but comparative case studies are needed to prove this.
- Technology has an important role to play in education, but the technologies chosen need to be appropriate for each specific school environment. Therefore, more research needs to be done to align the use of technology with the needs of schools, including not only learning spaces but also school planning and construction as well.
- There is also a need to generate evidence from infrastructure projects implemented in different contexts: from low to upper middle-income countries as well as from schools in different geographical locations, and with students from different cultural backgrounds.

Other specific topics that should be considered are:

- How to understand the potential for radically improving existing spaces through the creative use of fixtures and fittings and other low-budget adaptations of existing facilities to be able to teach in shifts if necessary.
- How to build long-term flexibility into physical infrastructure to accommodate future demographic and educational trends, while still meeting immediate needs.
- How schools can become beacons for education in their communities by opening access to most of their facilities but also by developing the outreach skills of teachers and pupils to provide education in the community, especially in remote rural locations.
- How to develop synergetic, harmonious designs that ensure that green and sustainable buildings can also be cost-effective learning environments (with comparative studies based on cost-benefit and lifecycle approaches).
- This list will remain open.

CONCLUSIONS

The overarching aspiration of this report has been to bring together the current evidence on the effects of education infrastructure design on students' outcomes. We found this evidence to be particularly strong on the impact of school planning and design on health and on the learning progress. Evidence on the impact of a good "fit" between pedagogy and school spaces was also highlighted. What has also become clear in our research is the importance of the related issues of educational quality, equality, coverage, purpose, and community engagement and of having an interdisciplinary dialogue on the implementation of infrastructure projects. We hope that this report will be a good start in helping those working on educational infrastructure investments to overcome the most common challenges and to reap all of the benefits that quality school infrastructure can bring to student achievement, teacher retention, and community satisfaction.

REFERENCE

UNESCO Institute for Statistics. 2012. *A Place to Learn: Lessons from Research on Learning Environments*. Montreal: UNESCO.

www.ingramcontent.com/pod-product-compliance
Lightning Source LLC
Chambersburg PA
CBHW060317240426

43661CB00059B/2795